Ethical Business Culture

Ethical Business Culture

A Utopia or a Challenge?

Andreas Karaoulanis

BEP

BUSINESS EXPERT PRESS

Leader in applied, concise business books

Ethical Business Culture: A Utopia or a Challenge?

Copyright © Business Expert Press, LLC, 2021.

Cover design by Charlene Kronstedt

Interior design by Exeter Premedia Services Private Ltd., Chennai, India

First published in 2021 by
Business Expert Press, LLC
222 East 46th Street, New York, NY 10017
www.businessexpertpress.com

ISBN-13: 978-1-95334-978-1 (paperback)
ISBN-13: 978-1-95334-979-8 (e-book)

Business Expert Press Entrepreneurship and Small Business Management Collection

Collection ISSN: 1946-5653 (print)
Collection ISSN: 1946-5661 (electronic)

First edition: 2021

10 9 8 7 6 5 4 3 2 1

Description

Small business is a major component of societies, especially now. Being in leadership positions in small business is something which many times involves tough decisions to be taken. The major question that this book addresses is whether ethical decision making in small business is a paragon that needs to be taken into consideration?

Surviving and growing is something which involves many aspects that need to be taken into consideration too. One of them is the human factor, which many consider to be a crucial paragon, more important than even strategy implementation. Under this prism, this book will investigate both the ethical paragons involved in small business ethical decision-making process and their consequences and the implementation of the right culture in small business as a paragon of stability and growth.

The author sheds some light into aspects that we all have encountered in our professional lives and which sometimes had major impact on both business and the environment.

Keywords

small business; management; crisis; financial; strategy; decision making; company culture; human paragon; human resources management; sustainable development; ethical consequences; ethical decision making; business ethics; morals; society; growth; CEO; leadership; conclusions; customers; value creation

Contents

Preface

A Few Words from the Author

As being someone who has worked for more than 25 years in more than 10 different industries, I believe that I have the experience to deal with a topic that, although well known, is something that the majority of businessmen/businesswomen and entrepreneurs don't like to touch.

Having ethical considerations while being an entrepreneur is not something easy. Many might argue that being an entrepreneur automatically means that you need to be ready to eliminate all second thoughts, especially when crucial; sometimes even for the business survival.

In this book I am trying to underline that entrepreneurs need to understand that business can be ethical or, in other words, business can implement principles like truthfulness, honesty, loyalty, respect, fairness, and integrity (Surbhi 2018) and still thrive. Ii is a matter of choice and understanding that businesses are part of the societies inside which they are operating and this is why they need to respect themselves, their employees, and the very societies of which they are a vivid part.

As a manager, CEO, and C-suite executive, in the past years I always wanted to implement a great company culture in all the companies that I was working. This fact per se was for me of the utmost importance because in the epicenter of business I always had the human factor in terms of both employees and customers. A human-centric approach, regarding personnel, combined with a customer-centric one can be a determinant which can be proved extremely crucial in terms of sustainability, customer retention, increase of profits, in both the short and the long runs.

As in small business it is imperative to understand the role of the owner (CEO) in implementing such business mentality; we also need to understand the role of the human resources as well. Human resource management can also be extremely important in terms of the ethical considerations that need to be addressed.

The bottom line is that business needs to operate under the prism of the open systems theory which states that business and society are interconnected in a way which creates very strong relationships that can affect them both negatively and positively. Businesses need to have in mind that they cannot survive if the society is devastated and this is something that needs to empower their corporate social responsibility actions. In addition, a positive company culture which makes people feel happy and fulfilled through their daily work assignments is imperative to be implemented as it can give to their company the competitive advantage needed in order to thrive.

These two pillars of ethical considerations need to be the drivers of all business decision making because otherwise we are going to have very negative results for both the business, in the long run, and the society in the short.

In the past, almost 10 years after the outbreak of the last global financial crisis, as many small businesses had to take crucial and quick decisions which affected their very survival, they forgot to scrutinize such decisions in terms of the ethical considerations that were lurking in the background. The result was that in many occasions local societies were devastated, while the local economies suffered and many families faced enormous problems in terms of their own survival. As such paradigms are indicative of why ethical decision making in small business is crucial, I wanted to grasp the opportunity to bring this important societal issue on the surface and to try to find ways to suggest new roads of collaboration between business and the society. Such collaborations can decrease such phenomena in the near future.

Acknowledgments

First and above all, I want to thank God who permitted me to continue with this book through the pandemic period in 2020. My family influenced my life more than anything else and this is why this book is dedicated to all of them too and especially to my kids. Thank you all and God bless you.

PART I

Business Ethics.
Is It a Prerequisite?

CHAPTER 1

What Do We Mean by Ethics?

Ethics: A General Description—Ethics or Morals?

Being a professional in any discipline usually results in tough decision making. Difficult circumstances are extremely possible to arise, circumstances which require, apart from a concrete technical and knowledge background, an inner mature personality which will be able to take the right decisions at the right point in time. Such decisions will not only be critical in terms of the very business, but also be very important in terms of creating or sustaining the right equilibrium inside the company and between the company and the surrounding society where the company in question operates.

But what do we mean by the term ethics and is there any kind of difference between ethics and morals, which is another term usually used in the same premises?

According to Surbhi (2018), ethics can be defined as follows: They are a philosophy which has to do with specific principles that can be used to describe the conduct between individuals or between a group and which can be used in order to help us decide what is good or bad. They can also be described as the standards which govern a person's life.

The principles that ethics involve are mainly the following:

- Truthfulness
- Honesty
- Loyalty
- Respect
- Fairness
- Integrity

(Surbhi 2018)

On the other hand, morals can be seen as the social, cultural, and religious beliefs or values of an individual or a group which can be used as a yardstick in order to help you determine what is right or wrong. They can be seen as the rules/standards that society usually imposes and which we are using in order to help us decide what is right or wrong in our everyday life (Surbhi 2018).

The more important principles of morals can be said to be the following:

- Do not cheat.
- Be loyal.
- Be patient.
- Always tell the truth.
- Be generous.
(Surbhi 2018)

It can be said that the Ten Commandments were the morals that God imposed to the Israeli, while ethics can be seen as the personal principles that everyone uses in order to define good or bad in one's life, especially when such principles are able to lead to the moral ones.

In Table 1.1 we can see the main differences between morals and ethics as Surbhi (2018) describes them.

A crucial point that will be examined throughout this book is the notion that "from the standpoint of moral philosophy, the idea of business ethics appears rather unusual" as Klikauer (2017) states in his paper titled "Business Ethics as Ideology?" The idea that business cannot be ethical is an idea that can be said to be a very natural one. Some might even argue that ethics and business have an oxymoron relationship somehow. But is that so? Is it impossible to have ethical business, especially nowadays?

The author of this book argues that, especially when we deal with small business, it is. A very characteristic example toward the same direction with the author of this book is what Fassin et al. (2011) discussed in their paper titled "Small-Business Owner-Managers' Perceptions of Business Ethics and CSR-Related Concepts." They stressed that given the impact that small business owners have in their very companies, both corporate social responsibility and company ethics can take

Table 1.1 Main differences between morals and ethics (Surbhi 2018)

Ethics	Morals
Ethics are dealing with what is "good or evil"	Morals are dealing with what is "right or wrong"
Ethics can describe one's reaction to a particular situation, For example, "Is it ethical to state the truth in a particular situation?"	Morals are general guidelines framed and implemented by the society, for example, "We should speak the truth"
Ethics is a word which originated from the ancient Greek word "ethikos" which refers to character	The term morals is derived from an ancient Greek word too, "mos" which refers to a specific custom which can be framed and implemented by a group of people and/or a public authority
Ethics are attributes of one's character and can be chosen by that very person	Morals can be dictated by the society, the culture, or the religion in this specific area
Ethics have to do with the right or wrong contact between individuals	Morals have to do with the principles that define what is good and what is not
When we refer to ethics, we need to understand that individuals are free to choose the principles that will govern their lives	Morals can be either accepted or rejected by the individuals as they are not responsible for them. The society is
Ethics are the same regardless of society, religion, or culture	Morals can vary from society to society, religion to religion, or culture to culture
Ethics can be widely seen in business where they are described as "business ethics"	Morals cannot be applied to business at all
Ethics cannot be expressed in the form of some kind of statement	Morals can be expressed in the form of statements

a different way in small business. The result can be that small business owners can be able to shape their company's culture in a very positive way and to implement ethical values that, although profit will always be their number one target, can be the cornerstone of their business' whole operations. This fact per se will have vast positive impact on the lives of the company's employees and in the long run to the societies in which these businesses are operating. But we will discuss extensively toward that direction in the chapters to come.

Ethics in Society and Business

Businesses are a part of society as they operate inside the society, they are influenced by it, and they influence it in a two-way interaction. This is what the open systems theory supports, which, according to Jung and Vakharia (2019), sees organizations as an opened and networked structure which is part of its external environment and is affected by it. Under this prism we can understand why morals can affect an organization's operation since they affect the ethics of the people who are working in that organization. In that way, depending on the location, the culture, and the religion of each society, organizations which are operating in it can be affected in a way that may influence deeply the company's culture.

Business can become quite tough sometimes, especially when the pursuit of increased ROI[1] can lead people to cross their ethics line. Meyer-Galow (2018) argues that business managers need to re-establish their reputation, since it has declined due to their disregard for moral decisions and the ethical practices that they might use.

According to Meyer-Galow (2018), business students during their studies are only taught about technical issues in order to acquire the knowledge needed to enter the industry. Such knowledge is not accompanied with compassion and a holistic engagement to business in order to shape an ethical behavior. This is why when entering the business field where they might be in the position to take difficult and hard decisions, they need to adapt a balanced behavior between business decision taking and ethics, something which is not part of their university training. Since their training involves only technical knowledge, they usually find themselves in a difficult position to balance their decisions with the demands of the ever-increasing profits (Meyer-Galow 2018).

Reputation which is equal to brand name is something that can be determined by its ethics (Skill and Esoft 2019). This is why having good business ethics is a paragon which is crucial for a company's sustainability and development. It is important for companies to be able to understand that if they will foster an ethical program and embed it in their business philosophy via the foundations of a successful company culture, they will be able to increase their profits and reach success (Skill and Esoft 2019). That will happen because the implementation of an ethical program will affect in a positive way not only the company's employees, but also their

---

[1] ROI: Return on investment.

customers, suppliers, competitors, and so on, and will therefore have a positive impact on society as a whole (Skill and Esoft 2019). This is why ethical business has tremendous positive results to business and society and, although some may refer to it as trivial, in reality it has huge dynamics and can be the cornerstone of every profitable business.

On the other hand, what is equally important to understand is that the influence of company ethics on company's employees and its surrounding society is not a one-way road, as the influence goes both ways. Customers, suppliers, competitors, and so on can also input some positive influence on the company as well by returning this positive reaction (Skill and Esoft 2019).

Imagine that only a few years ago, the reputation of a company had to do with magazines, the news, and customers' opinion which could mainly be spread in the area that they were living or working. Although it was also very important to keep customers satisfied in order to achieve retention and a good brand name, today, things are quite different. Customers have the power to create an instant online word of mouth which can reach hundreds of thousands of others in just a second. This huge power they have is a determinant on how companies need to perceive their interaction with their customers. Since company ethics have, as we saw, a two-way positive interaction with clients, imagine what can happen if that interaction becomes a negative one. It is inevitable that the company's reputation can easily suffer a huge damage.

We understand from the above that company ethics are very important because not only can they shape the lives of thousands that interact with the company, but also they are a huge business determinant that can make business flourish or destroy very easily.

Business ethics are very important, as we saw, in terms of how businesses consider their involvement to society. We are all witnessing the huge environmental problem that our planet is facing. We all know that this problem was mainly created due to a bad approach that businesses have, on a global scale, toward environment. If business managers are not able to take ethical decisions that affect the environment, they need to understand, since organizations are open systems, that the consequences will be vast not only for the societies and the business itself, but also for them and the generations to come.

Another way that business activities can negatively influence the surrounding society is when businesses via their nonethical decision taking are disturbing the social stability, causing huge social problems to regions or even to entire countries (Aßländer and Goessling 2017). The example of Greece and other European countries, which suffered from the last financial crisis which of course was the result of business activities in a fragile global society, is indicative of such negative influence. It is also a characteristic example of how business ethics can impact the macro-level of the social web (Aßländer and Goessling 2017).

Human Resources as the Go-Between

Employment standards are crucial in any business as they are the cornerstone for the building of a good team which will promote business and thus customer retention and therefore ROI.

Human resource management can be seen as the connecting link between the head of the company (e.g., the CEO) who is responsible for the implementation of a specific company culture and the personnel. In addition, human resource management can be seen as the connecting link between companies and the surrounding community where the business in question operates in terms of defining this very way of interaction based on specific ethical standards that are posed by the company via, for example, the company culture. How ethical is the human resource management is quite crucial for the business and this is why ethical human resource management is going to be a developing theme over the next few years (Winstanley et al. 1996).

The interest on business ethics has increased in the last years throughout the world due to the increased understanding from all businessmen that they are extremely important for their business via their necessity in all business functions and particularly in human resource management (Al-Tarawneh 2020). This is why the role of human resource management seems very important nowadays. Human resource handling the company's personnel is something that will have vast impact in the company's performance toward the acquisition of the holy grail of all business, the gain of the competitive advantage needed in order to make business flourish.

Having the above in mind and since we are discussing about humans, it is imperative to understand that creating a high morale in business is something that vastly has to do with ethical considerations. Therefore, human resource management involves several practices that should be based on ethical principles like the ones we described earlier (fairness, honesty, respect, etc.) (Al-Tarawneh 2020).

This is why research (Al-Tarawneh 2020) indicated that there is a high degree of commitment between business ethics and human resource management practices (Al-Tarawneh 2020). All procedures that human resource needs to follow as part of its job description, like recruitment, selection, training, compensation, and appraisal of employees' performance, need to be committed with the implementation of the right business ethics (Al-Tarawneh 2020); otherwise the whole business culture will collapse and the result will be devastating for the business itself in both the short and the long run.

Human resources managers usually have to face the following dilemma: Should they need to focus on the human factor based on solid moral and ethical grounds or exclusively focus on the money quantifiable performance (Cătălina 2008)? There are times when human resource management needs to understand that having employees who are committed to results only is not a panacea toward success. Employees with high ethical standards can make a difference and can be the cornerstone upon which the company can build its future performance and its increased ROI. Of course, the combination of both is ideal, but we need to understand that when leadership is important, ethical values are the ones that will determine the future of the business in the long run. Examples of such situations can be seen in every business small or big.

The advent of AI (Artificial Intelligence) will leave no choice to small business owners but to focus on their human resources because they will not be able to compete their big, probably global rivals which will have the economic resources to use AI to acquire their needed competitive advantage, and so they will need to focus on their people and their soft skills like leadership, decision making, and team building. Company culture can also play a crucial role toward that direction. So, human resources need to understand their new role and also that they need to become the missing link between that role and the company owner because otherwise they will not be able to implement such ethical base in their business.

Employees are basic stakeholders for a company; customers are too and since we need to see the whole business perspective, we need to understand that business operates via the use of employees toward creating value for its customers. Since, according to the stakeholder theory, stakeholders are crucial players in the "business game," they need to be taken under vast consideration. The stakeholder theory states that "the purpose of a business is to create value for both stakeholders and shareholders. Any business need to consider customers, suppliers, employees, communities and shareholders as well" (stakeholdermap.com n.d.).

Human resources management needs to understand the danger that the upper company management usually faces, a danger which has to do with its focus primarily on the financial success and the reach of their personal and company goals in several dimensions that involve their business presence, like operational quality, financial strategy, workforce motivation, and cost-cutting strategies, while they tend to neglect a crucial paragon which is the company's social responsibility and the human factor in their business which involves their employees and the company's customers (Ogunyemi 2013). Since this kind of behavior is the one that will bring the company into facing difficult circumstances, in both the short and long runs, the human resources management needs to connect the dots and fill such a potential gap as well.

Another issue that might seek the attention of the human resources department is that sometimes companies have to face markets where the posed rules are unclear and the majority of the companies operating in such markets need to "play the game" for survival by following such unclear rules and paths. This fact per se makes the whole decision-making process very difficult and really poses the threat of not following standard ethical approaches.

As we saw in previous paragraphs, business ethics are vital for both the business and the society. Ethical leadership can be seen as the cornerstone for the implementation of the right company ethics, while another key element which can bridge the ethical gap between the decision maker, the employees, the management, and the society in terms of the implementation of the organizational business ethics is the human resources department (Hulpke and Lau 2008).

So, it is obvious from the above that the role of human resource management is crucial when it comes to business ethics and its impact on both organizational and societal levels. As the human resources is the department which is in the hands of the decision makers on an organizational level, it is its responsibility to implement the company culture and to impose the unwritten laws that are running throughout the company as the company's informal organization. We can see the differences between formal and informal organizations and the key elements of both in Table 1.2.

We can easily understand that an informal organization involves many ethical characteristics that the people who are working in the company follow. This kind of informal organization cannot be implemented in the right way without the support of the human resources department. If the informal organization is a good one which creates a good work spirit that is both ethical and easy to live with, then we are talking about a healthy organization. Of course, we always need to remember that the company's formal organization is equally important. The common point is that for both the organizations, the human resources department has to play a crucial role.

A key element in terms of the role of the human resources department in bridging the gap between the company's ethics, the employees, and the society is the relationship between the department and the company's board of directors or the CEO or both. Since CEOs are mainly focused on achieving financial targets, they might miss the bottom line which is that a great company culture and corporate social responsibility are the paragons that will bring prosperity to the company in the long run. The role of the human resources department is to close this very gap by creating a trust relationship with the CEO and remind the CEO about that very bottom line. Since, especially in small business, the ethical considerations on organizational level usually spring from the company's owner who usually is the company's CEO, such considerations, in case they are forgotten, need to be reminded by the human resources team.

Table 1.2 Comparison between formal and informal organizations (Keydifferencies.com 2017)

Basis for comparison	Formal organization	Informal organization
Meaning	An organization type in which the job of each members is clearly defined, whose authority, responsibility, and accountability are fixed in formal organization	An organization formed within the formal organization as a network of interpersonal relationship when people interact with each other is known as informal organization
Creation	Deliberately by top management	Spontaneously by members
Purpose	To fulfill the ultimate objective of the organization	To satisfy their social and psychological needs
Nature	Stable; continuous for a long time	Unstable
Communication	Official communication	Grapevine
Control mechanism	Rules and regulation	Norms, values, and beliefs
Focus on	Work performance	Interpersonal relationship
Authority	Members are bound by hierarchical structure	All members are equal
Size	Large	Small

Another important element of human resources role in terms of the company's ethical values is that they have the opportunity to play a greater role than the one with which they were assigned in order to be able to contribute to the company's overall success in a more dynamic way which is based on ethics and values (Caldwell et al. 2010; 2011). They can develop systems and policies, based on their knowledge and experience, which will be aligned with the company's values, mission, and vision (Caldwell et al. 2010; 2011). This suggests that the human resources' role has many ethical implications regarding the organization in which they operate.

As they are responsible for the personnel of the company in terms of recruiting and dealing with all the issues that might arise inside the company during its operations, it is imperative to have an ethical dimension and to seek excellence based upon an ethical base.

Caldwell et al. (2010; 2011) first introduced the model of "ethical stewardship" which can be translated into a model of governance that honors obligations due to the many stakeholders inside and around an organization and which maximizes the company's long-term wealth creation. If human resources will be able to adapt to such framework in addition to a transformative leadership profile, this fact per se will be able to assist them in realizing their ethical responsibilities to a greater extent and will make them even more effective in helping the company in which they operate to achieve its goals (Caldwell et al. 2010; 2011).

As Manroop et al. (2014) state in their research, human resource systems are a very important influencing paragon regarding the company's performance via the development of specific resources that are deeply in alignment with the company's historical background and general culture. In simple words, human resources are the lever via which the leader/CEO/owner of the company implements a culture which is aligned with that person's values, ideas, and ethics.

But what happens when a human resources executive understands that such implementation is not going to have a positive impact on the company's culture as it is expressed via, for example, an unethical leadership by, for example, the company's owner? It is the time for responsibility, and human resources executives have the privilege and responsibility to suggest systems and practices that will help the company toward the implementation of an ethical company culture. They can be seen as catalysts while their role is of utmost importance and this is why they need to be ethical elements and people with character and bold enough to risk their position if needed for the general good.

A survey research that was conducted by Bartels et al. (1998) among 1,078 human resources managers resulted in a statistically significant negative relationship between the strength of a company's ethical climate and the seriousness of ethical violations that occur. In simple words, the more ethical the company's culture was, the less severe the ethical violations were. On the other hand, the research uncovered a statistically significant positive correlation between a company's ethical culture and success in terms of responding to the potential ethical issues that might arise (Barters et al. 1998).

Such results come to underline the need for interventions toward the strengthening of the company's ethical culture in order to help management to handle ethical issues inside the company (Barters et al. 1998). If we combine the results of this research with the role of the human resource executives as was stressed in the previous paragraphs, we can understand that the role of the human resources in strengthening an ethical climate/company culture inside the company is paramount and that all human resources professionals need to understand that this role should be a prerequisite in terms of their skills that correspond to their position. The human resource management plays a vital role not only in shaping the company's culture but also in creating an ethical climate toward ethical decision making from the higher levels of hierarchy.

From the above, we can understand the importance of the human resources department in terms of both the organizational ethics and the company's corporate social responsibility. The human resources influence on the CEO's decision making is also crucial and can alter the whole scenery for any business.

Author's Notes

This chapter mainly discussed general meanings regarding ethics and morals, small business and their correlation with the society and the business in general and the role of the human resources team in building an ethical company culture as the go-between the personnel on the one side and the company's head on the other.

The main focus of the chapter was on the correlation between business and society via the prism of the open systems theory. Corporate social responsibility needs to be underlined as the cornerstone of all business, since nobody can thrive and sustain in terms of doing business in a devastating society where she will need to operate.

The following topics need to be discussed:

- Ethics and morals: key differences and similarities
- Corporate social responsibility
- Open systems theory

- Stakeholders theory (just a few introductory words as it will be discussed in the chapters to follow)
- Human resources as the missing link in connecting or not connecting ethical companies with their employees

Questions

1. What are the main differences between ethics and morals?
2. What is the definition of corporate social responsibility? Why it is important for both the company and the society as a whole?
3. What does the open systems theory dictate?
4. What does the stakeholders theory dictate? What is its correlation to the corporate social responsibility?
5. What is the role of human resources in terms of connecting companies with its workforce under the ethical company culture prism?

CHAPTER 2

Decision Making in Small Business

Small Business' Main Characteristics

We discussed about small business without really knowing what small businesses are. As in European Union (EU) recommendation 2003/361 (ec.europa.eu n.d. cited in Karaoulanis 2017), the key characteristics that can be used in order to let us understand if a business can be seen as small or not are the company's staff headcount and either turnover or balance sheet total (ec.europa.eu n.d. cited in Karaoulanis 2017). Table 2.1 gives us a very vivid depiction of this very recommendation.

Another very important element that we need to have in mind is that as Gama et al. (2012 cited in Karaoulanis 2017; p. 3130) indicates, "99% of the economic activities in the EU can be traced back to SMEs. This accounts to the two thirds of all jobs in the private sector." This fact per se is indicative of the importance of small businesses for every market in which they operate and most of all, for every society. Problems that small businesses might face can have vast impact on the surrounding society inside which they operate. As we spontaneously discussed in Chapter 1,

Table 2.1 Factors determining whether a company can be characterized as small business or not (ec.europa.eu n.d. cited in Karaoulanis 2017)

Company category	Staff headcount	Turnover	Balance sheet total
Medium-sized	<250	≤50 million €	≤43 million €
Small	<50	≤10 million €	≤10 million €
Micro	<10	≤2 million €	≤2 million €

the open systems theory, which stresses that organizations need to be seen as an open and networked structure which is part of and affected by the external environment and vice versa (Jung and Vakharia 2019), in combination with the above is leading us to the logical conclusion that small business is a vital part of the society with which it interacts. According to open systems theory, small businesses have a vast impact, positive or negative, on societal level in multiple ways. On the other hand, societal problems can affect small business in a very straight forward and vital way.

Another very important characteristic of small business which is also extremely important and defines the company's overall performance and sustainability over the years is that small business owners are quite different than entrepreneurs, at least in the way that economic models and policy makers often have in mind (Hurst et al. 2011). Under this prism, Hurst et al. (2011) argue that, according to their research, only few small business owners intend to disrupt the market in which they operate by bringing a fresh idea on the table or are ready to enter a new market or create a new one. The big majority of them intend to serve an existing market via the use of an existing service. It can be said somehow that small business owners are more conservative (Hurst et al. 2011).

Another crucial point, which over the years has become an important characteristic of small business, is that small business owners need to answer the question "what should I do with my business? Should I grow it big and innovate, or should I stay small?" (Hurst et al. 2011). This is an extremely important question which defines the future of the small business in question in a very crucial way. Hurst et al. (2011) also argue that the usual answer to that question is that "we don't want to grow our business big" and this fact per se has to mainly do with the small business industry which is concentrated around skilled craftspeople, lawyers, real estate agents, health care providers, small shopkeepers, and so on (Hurst et al. 2011).

Another characteristic of small business which springs from the research of Hurst et al. (2011) is that benefits like, being your own boss, having flexibility of hours, and social status, of being an entrepreneur are decision paragons toward the non-expansion of small business. Small business owners tend to feel comfortable in their jobs and standard of living and this is something that sometimes makes them not to decide to expand and stop being small (Hurst et al. 2011). Another paragon toward that decision is the fact that nowadays, especially after the last Covid-19 pandemic, small business owners feel very insecure, something which makes them not determined enough to leave their comfort zone.

Similarly an important characteristic of small business has to do with the way such businesses approach the stakeholder theory. We discussed about the stakeholder theory in the previous chapter, but the way small business operates inside the boundaries of this very theory is something unique which defines its course of action and operational decisions as well. According to Lähdesmäki et al. (2019), the stakeholder salience process for small businesses is a paragon which is influenced by the degree to which they are embedded in the societies in which they operate. This way of influencing has to do with the way that small business owners socialize. In other words, small business owners have multiple relationships with their company's stakeholders beyond their business context. This fact per se is something unique for small business, especially for the ones that operate in small societies, and does not happen in larger businesses which have a different way of approaching their stakeholders on societal level as they mainly exercise their corporate social responsibility toward that direction.

The social proximity that can be seen between small business owners and the business stakeholders is a very important paragon which is not only shaping the business' commercial strategy, but also the decision-making process and the ethical standards that the company exercises as part of its company culture.

Another characteristic which shapes the decision-making process, not only in small businesses, is their financing. As we said in the previous paragraphs, small business is the backbone of all societies and a vital component of all the markets in which it operates; especially nowadays due to the presence of Internet, they are operating in a global market, in many ways. This very importance of small businesses on a global level in addition to their proximity with the local societies, as can be seen through the lens of the stakeholder and the open systems theory, makes their financing a very important parameter which can have vast implications not only for the business but for the society as whole. Small businesses can be globally characterized as economically frustrated as they usually face important difficulties in accessing formal finance in comparison with the difficulties that large companies also face (Berger and Udell 2006, cited in Karaoulanis 2017). The majority of small businesses are mainly based on their internal finance (i.e., owner's capitals and/or loans and retained earnings) (Zairis 2015, cited in Karaoulanis 2017).

This characteristic is a very crucial one and can be involved in many ways with the decision-making process, with the answer to ethical dilemmas that might appear, and with the small business' corporate social responsibility, especially when such small business operates in small societies.

Another important characteristic of small business that needs to be discussed is that it is usually uncertainty averse. According to Vlaar et al. (2006, cited in Karaoulanis 2017), when uncertainty increases, small business tends to focus more on processes and structures that point to more systematic task execution. This is the result of its effort toward the minimization of the error margin in its processes which finally leads to fewer errors in the decision-making process. Uncertainty avoidance can be seen as a small business characteristic which sometimes has a positive impact on small businesses as it tends to organize them more, but, on the other hand, as we already discussed, makes them less convenient with changes and with the idea that one day they will grow large. No doubt that this is a characteristic that, at least to some extent, has to do with the small business owners' mentality and approach to both business and life.

Hofstede et al. (2010, p. 191) stressed that uncertainty avoidance can be described as "the extent to which the members of a culture feel threatened by ambiguous or unknown situations. This feeling is, among other manifestations, expressed through nervous stress and in a need for predictability: a need for written and unwritten rules." This is why in strong uncertainty avoidance societies, people prefer to base their business and lives on a structured environment which is surrounded by formal laws, rules, and regulations in a way to decrease uncertainty and errors. As Hofstede et al. (2010) indicates, such behavior is something that is programmed since people's early childhood, so we can easily understand why small business owners' mentality has to do a lot with the uncertainty avoidance that small businesses show. Of course this is not the only reason, as their liquidity problems are a strong indicator toward feeling uncertain.

Having in mind that a very large proportion of small businesses are family owned, we need to understand that such ownership usually adapts different approaches than the ones that we encounter in larger corporations. This specific family logic is responsible for shaping managerial practices in small business to a great extent (Brundin et al. 2014). This kind of ownership (family-owned small business) is a category of ownership which has specific characteristics which as Brundin et al. (2014) stress are the following: active, visible, and persistent ownership with few owners, relatively stable strategic development encompassing multiple ownership goals, autonomy toward capital markets, and a strong identification and emotional bonding with the business. Such characteristics can be found in the majority of small businesses. Their combination with the small business' interaction with the local societies or the bond that small business owners have with their stakeholders, especially when such businesses operate in small societies, is a paragon which overall shapes the small business' way of operating in many ways, one of which is business ethics, something that we will discuss in the following chapter.

The Decision-Making Process

Decision making is a procedure and as such, can be depicted via the several steps that are followed in order to reach a conclusion.

An important element of the whole decision-making process is that businesses, in order to reach such conclusions/decisions, need to use information which will come from within the company, from outside the company, or both. So when we have to decide for something internal, for example, how to improve our customer service, it is vital that we use information from both inside and outside the company. We need our valued customers' opinions regarding our services, but we also need to take a look at our internal processes and of course to check our KPIs.[1]

According to Purwati et al. (2014), there is always the other side of the coin. Companies struggle to take the right decisions for everyday issues

---

[1] Key performance indicator (KPI) is a measurable value that demonstrates how effectively a company is in achieving key business objectives. Organizations use KPIs at multiple levels to evaluate their success at reaching targets. High-level KPIs may focus on the overall performance of the business, while low-level KPIs may focus on processes in departments such as sales, marketing, HR, and support (klipfolio.com n.d.).

at work. Such decisions might have important implications for the whole company. For example, investors need information regarding the business conditions, which will help them accordingly to reach a decision regarding investing or not in the company in question, as information plays a critical role for all companies regarding their decision-making process.

Apart from the importance of information in terms of decision making, another critical factor is the use of several steps that will be followed throughout the process of decision making in order to make it more efficient and of course more easily monitored. This efficiency has to do with an easier and more accessible and understandable way to implement the process in question, something which, generally speaking, results in more viable and "to the target" results.

Jocumsen (2004) identifies, via his research, three steps or tasks that are forming a decision-making process:

1. Information gathering/research
2. Financial analyses and assessments
3. Internal matters (Jocumsen 2004)

These steps are supported by key "methods" which are used in carrying out them and which are classified into learned competencies, inherent competencies, internal networks, and external networks (Jocumsen 2004).

According to cliffnotes.com (n.d.), the decision-making process involves several steps given in Table 2.2.

You can't solve a problem which is not well defined and framed. This is the most important step as it can be seen as the cornerstone upon which the whole process is being built. Several ways can be used in that direction; one very interesting is the root-cause analysis.[2] Put in simple words, you need to know which is the root of the problem in hand in order to solve it once and for all.

In the whole decision-making process another very important parameter that need to be taken under consideration are the so called "limiting

---

[2] Root-cause analysis is a method which is conducted in order to identify the origin of each error (Cohen et al. 2010).

Table 2.2 Steps in the decision-making process (cliffnotes.com n.d.)

Define the problem
Identify limiting factors
Develop potential alternatives
Analyze the alternatives
Select the best alternative
Implement the decision
Establish a control and evaluation system

factors." According to ukessays.com (2018), a limiting factor is any factor that restricts a company from its activities. Such factors can be labor time, raw material, machine hours, space for inventory, and so on. In order to understand the role that limiting factors play for a company, let's imagine a sales team which needs, for example, 10,000 items due to demand in the market. The company's capacity in terms of producing such items is, for example, 5,000 pieces.

It is obvious that there is a gap between demand and supply. Such gap can be the result of several paragons; the most common one is the use of specific resources needed to produce the product. Let's now say that such resource is iron; then we have a scarce resource which is the iron. In our case, iron can be seen as the limiting factor regarding our production and satisfaction of the demand of our customers. In our decision making, for example, in order to create a blue print of our strategy, our scarce resource (iron) will be a constraint, a limiting factor which will inevitably send us toward a different direction from the one that we would have taken if it wasn't scarce. We realize from this example how vital it is to know and handle accordingly our limiting factors and to understand how important their involvement is in the decision-making process.

Another important step in the decision-making process is the development of potential alternative solutions to our problem that we struggling to solve. Such alternatives are crucial because they are giving us the options to adapt in order to solve our problem and not reach a dead end. Developing alternatives is very important as they can give us the opportunity to reach decisions in a more unbiased and less stressful way.

But adapting such alternatives is not something that we have to take loosely. We need to analyze them in order to select the best one, which can be the solution to our problem. Such analysis needs to take into consideration many paragons like the character of the alternative and how it is compatible with our problem and in general with our company's direction and way of seeing things. It also needs to consider its special characteristics in order to avoid creating any kind of conflict with other areas of our business.

If we continue with the problem of the scarce iron that we introduced earlier, we can understand that if we offer an alternative solution to increase, for example, the capacity of our factory to produce more iron and reach our customers' demand, then we will probably create a problem to other departments or other resources that are used in the production phase as we are going to spend a bigger part of our budget to cover such a demand, something which means that we probably won't be able to support another department or another demand. Of course this is something that can occur, but it is also something that has to do with the commercial strategy that our company has in mind to implement or has already implemented.

What is most important here is to understand that our goal is always to choose the best alternative between the ones we have on the table. This is our goal and of course our next step after the alternatives' analysis.

What is also crucial and needs our attention in detail is that after we reach a decision regarding which alternative is the best solution for our problem, we need to implement our decision on an operational level. Such implementation is not easy and we have to take under consideration several factors like whether the whole process is in conformity with our operational process, how should we need to implement our decision, which persons/teams are involved, and do we have any time limitations? In other words, we need to implement a project which is vital for the problem's solution. This project can be a small or a bigger one and can be simple or can involve many time limitations (matrix organizations[3]).

Equally important after the implementation phase is that we need to establish a control and evaluation system. In simple words, a system

---

[3] Matrix organization: This kind of structure is the most complex one and it is mainly used in companies which handle large-scale projects. By this structure, we have more than one line of reporting managers. In simple words, each employee needs to be accountable to more than one boss, for example, to the project manager and to the functional (i.e., department) manager (corporatefinanceinstitute.org. (2) n.d.).

which will enable us to have control over the implementation of the above-mentioned steps and monitor them in order to be able to evaluate them and identify potential flaws that might occur in order to be able to fix them. Systems that are usually used in such occasions are the ERP[4] ones.

Another important aspect of the decision-making process is that we always need to have in mind that the decisions taken throughout such processes can affect business critically. As such decisions are critical for any business, it is more than obvious that business owners and managers need to rely on decision components that seem at least solid enough to become the foundations of their decisions. Ghattas et al. (2014) under-line that the criteria used in such decision-making processes are not always formally specified and optimized. They also stress that when you are about to implement the decision-making process, you need to identify a process path that would be possible to yield the best possible performance for your business at a given context (Ghattas et al. 2014).

The above-mentioned authors describe an approach which uses data mining techniques to help the decision makers to identify the possible relationships between the existing context, the decision path, and, of course, the outcome of the whole process. Continuing, this whole process that gives us the above-mentioned relationships is used per se to help the decision makers to form decision rules that are vital for the final out-come (Ghattas et al. 2014). Additionally, decision makers step into the evaluation part of the whole process by the use of a simulation of the manufacturing process, the results of which depict the potential that exist in terms of improving the whole business performance through the rules that they generated, as we saw, via this whole approach/process (Ghattas et al. 2014).

It is very important to understand that decision making has various impacts, positive or not, in terms of not only the process that we are

---

[4] Enterprise resource planning (ERP) is a process used by companies to manage and integrate the important parts of their businesses. Many ERP software applica-tions are important to companies because they help them implement resource plan-ning by integrating all of the processes needed to run their companies with a single system. An ERP software system can also integrate planning, purchasing inventory, sales, marketing, finance, human resources, and more (investopedia n.d.).

following, but also the output of our business. This is why Mustafa et al. (2004) stress that there is an urgent industrial need to not only investigate the manufacturing options that can be seen as the result of a specific decision-making process, but also to gauge the impact of the decision making in terms of the economic results and the process perspectives. On the same wavelength Barjzktarović et al. (2019) are underlying in their research that it is of the outmost importance that we need decision makers and/or business owners to understand the connection between the decisions made and the financial result. This is something extremely crucial as it may be indicative that something needs to be changed in terms of the very decision-making process under specific circumstances.

Gavin (2020), in his article titled "8 Steps in the Decision-Making Process" in Harvard Business School Online, underlines the importance of understanding the decision-making process and presents it as a vital asset that all managers should have in their possession. He stresses that honing your approach to decision making is something that can potentially boost your job performance and give you the skill set that you need to advance your career. This is indicative of the importance of the decision-making process itself (Gavin 2020).

The decision-making process has multiple positive outcomes in both business and managers. The monitoring of its economic impact is huge and it is a paragon that needs to be taken under vast consideration as it can yield positive or negative results to the whole business. Managers and decision makers in general can benefit by understanding and improving this whole process, which in both the short and the long runs will prove beneficial for the business and of course for the customers as the right decision making will add value to them as well.

In small business, a real problem is the lack of internal processes that are deep and effective and usually the majority of the decision making left to be done by the company's owner. This fact per se is usually the result of a pathogen as small business owners usually take decisions based on their instincts and experience and they do not feel the need for the adoption of a specific process toward that decision making. This has to change in order to increase dramatically the success of the decision making, which, as we discussed in the previous paragraph, will have a positive monetary impact on their whole business. But this is something that has to do a lot with the owner's mentality and her adoption capability and desire, things that we will discuss further in Chapter 3.

Strategy Formulation and Decision Making in Small Business

In small business the decision making usually comes directly from the head of the company, or, in other words, from the company's owner. In several small businesses the business itself is owned by the family and the family members are the ones responsible for the decision making.

We can easily understand that when it comes to small business and especially to the family-owned ones, things are becoming a bit different. Not only does the decision making springs directly from the head (e.g., from the owner-father if it is a family-owned company), but the strategic decisions and the strategy implementation are also in the responsibility area of the same person. So, what is the connection between decision making and strategy formulation and implementation in small business? Are these two vital paragons interconnected and if yes how and to what degree? These are some of the questions that we will try to answer in this part of the book in order to get a better understanding of the mechanisms involved in the decision-making process and their ethical consequences and implications.

According to Brouthers et al. (1998), strategic decisions are of the utmost importance for both big and small companies. Taking the right decision given the specific circumstances and time frame can be a decisive paragon, which can make the difference between success and failure in business (Brouthers et al. 1998).

An important characteristic found widely in small business is that, as the CEO/owner of the company is responsible for the decision making, her main characteristics that are important regarding the decision-making process play an important role in terms, for example, of international strategic decision-making process and specifically in terms of international market selection and entry mode selection (Musso and Francioni 2012). One of the most important of these characteristics that influence the operations that we mentioned above is the CEO's educational background (Musso and Francioni 2012).

According to a research conducted in Australia on 13 case studies of Australian SMEs, in terms of strategic decision making, a weakness that was found had to do with SMEs' owners' narrow focus in developing potential decision alternatives (Hang and Wang 2012).

Another study that examined the effects of CEO gender on market orientation, which of course includes strategic decision making and performance and accordingly growth and profitability and used a sample of small and medium businesses which were operating in the service industry, found that gender plays a very important role (Davis et al. 2010). The research indicated that female-led service-oriented SMEs performed significantly better than the male-led ones due to their stronger market orientation because such firms were able to transmit better their market performance into a financial one. So, gender can be a decisive paragon as well in terms of the characteristics of the small business' CEO regarding the company's orientation toward a specific strategic decision making.

On the same wavelength, Sonfield et al. (2001) conducted a research on a U.S. national sample of 184 small business owners comprising 59 percent males and 41 percent females. The results indicated that there is no significant difference when it comes to gender especially in terms of venture innovation, risk taking, and strategic formulation and implementation that was chosen by the above-mentioned business owners (Sonfield et al. 2001).

Several researches keep searching in order to find a potential correlation between SMEs' CEOs' specific characteristics and how they exercise their strategic decision in their business in terms of both strategy formulation and strategy implementation. It is important here to notice that the decision-making process is usually set, in SMEs, by the CEO/owner of the company and this is why it is important to understand which ones of their characteristics are the ones that have an important impact in the company's strategy. The main reason for considering the importance of this factor is because strategy formulation can be vital for the company's sustainability in both the short and the long run.

In accordance with the above, Karami et al. (2006) conducted a research to examine the role of SMEs' CEOs in the formulation and deployment of the company's business strategy. The above-mentioned researchers examined the hypothesis that there is a kind of relationship between CEOs' age, work experiences, educational background, their company's strategy formulation, and the impact of their strategic awareness on their part upon firm's performance. The research sample included 508 SMEs in the electronics industry and the method included self-reported rating survey questionnaire and interviews which gave to the researchers 132 completed responses and 12 in-depth interviews (Karami et al. 2006). The results of the research showed that there was only trivial correlation between the CEOs' age and their performance strategy, while experience, which was another characteristic examined, placed more emphasis on formal strategy development. The CEOs' strategic awareness and knowledge regarding its importance and how markets work were found to play a very important role in the formulation of the company's business strategic movements. Finally, the CEOs' educational background was found to be the springboard toward the company's formal strategy development (Karami et al. 2006).

In another research conducted in China among SMEs and via the use of 289 valid questionnaires by Wu et al. (2017), the results indicated that the risk perceptions of the SMEs' top management team (TMT)—which included the company's CEO and her family, in case of a family-owned company, or the CEO and the company's top management team—and their mental models, which serve the company as a mediating factor, were affected by their characteristics and of course by their decision-making attitude (Wu et al. 2017). The same research also found that psychological ownership exerts moderating effects on the characteristics of the members of the TMT and their decision making (Wu et al. 2017).

Author's Notes

In this chapter we discussed about what small businesses are in terms of their characteristics and how they can be distinguished from other larger ones. We also discussed about the decision-making process on a general basis and we stressed the steps that we need to follow in order to reach our decision. Finally we saw how strategy formulation and decision making are interconnected with the CEO's characteristics in small business management.

The following topics need to be discussed:

- Which business can be called "small business"? Why? How can they be distinguished from larger ones?
- Why can small business, although they are small, play a huge role on societal level?
- Which main steps comprise the decision-making process? Which of them are crucial and are there any kind of interdependencies between them?
- How are decision making and strategy formulation interconnected with the company's CEO's personal characteristics and mentality?

Questions

1. Why does the small business play a vital role in the society as a whole?
2. Why is the small business CEO's mentality crucial for the company's performance and the company's strategy formulation?
3. The decision-making process can be analyzed in separate steps that need to be followed. If yes, are they interconnected and how?

CHAPTER 3

Ethical Consequences Involved in Small Business Decision Making

Decision Making and Ethical Parameters

Small business owners and entrepreneurs in general in their daily operations need to decide over ambiguous and complex situations (Busenitz and Barney 1997, cited in Dunham et al. 2008). Moreover, another very important point is that when decision makers need to reach a decision they usually need to face many ethical tensions resulting from the so many moral considerations and their potential consequences that arise from the entrepreneurial action itself (Dees and Starr 1992, cited in Dunham et al. 2008).

Decision making can be a tricky and difficult. Usually, during the process of actually taking the decision there are several parameters that need to be examined. One of them is to understand the ethical weight of such a decision via the potential impact it might have on the company's stakeholders and the society as a whole. Especially nowadays decisions can have vast impact on the whole world as, for example, environmental issues might arise if they do not follow the ethical path and do not bear in mind the interests of the company's stakeholders.

In such occasions, as Caughron et al. (2011) indicates, when it comes to decision making, companies usually follow specific reasoning strategies. Such strategies can be influenced by environmental factors and in return they might influence sense making, which might influence the ethical decision making.

But another important parameter that gets involved in decision making in terms of its ethical dimensions is employees' moral disengagement.

Such parameter is crucial and can lead to difficult circumstances that might shake the environment and the equilibrium inside the company. Of course, if we are going to reach such levels of moral disengagement it is a strong indicator that our company culture has somehow collapsed.

But let's discuss a bit about moral disengagement. Empathy and moral identity are factors that are negatively related to moral disengagement (Detert et al. 2008). On the other hand the negative factors which are positively related to moral disengagement are trait cynicism and chance locus of control orientation (Detert et al. 2008). What is very interesting here is that if moral disengagement is the case then unethical decision making will very probably appear in the company (Detert et al. 2008).

An ethical company culture, for example, a servant leadership and a role model management by the small business owner, can be seen as a deterrent paragon which can decrease or even prevent moral disengagement inside the company. As such it can become a barrier toward unethical decision making.

Ethical decision making is something that cannot be examined without taking into consideration parameters like the external environment, the ethical mindset of the CEO who is responsible for both the decision making and the implementation of an ethical company culture, as well as the time frame in which the whole scenario is taking place.

It is imperative to understand that when companies are facing, for example, fiscal difficulties in the societies in which they are operating, decision makers are more tempted in unethical decision making in order to survive and save their business. Under this prism, Onu et al. (2018; 2019) conducted a research on the behavior of 300 small business owners in terms of assessing the role of internalized motivation to pay taxes versus the extrinsic motivation in driving their business toward tax compliance. According to this study, internalized and extrinsic motivations have distinct predictors (Onu et al. 2018; 2019). On the one hand, internalized motivation is related to strong personal moral norms to comply and a sense that the fiscal system is fair toward everybody. Decision makers who had that internalized motivation were more likely to take ethical decisions, for example, in our case in terms of paying their taxes (Onu et al. 2018; 2019). On the other hand, extrinsic motivation was found to be related to personal perceptions that governmental laws in terms of penalties, checks, and so on were severe and likely to happen, while, in many such cases, it was found that decision makers suffered a lack of knowledge relevant to the taxes mechanisms (Onu et al. 2018; 2019). In such occasions, the decision makers were more likely to take the decision to evade tax payment, a decision which can be considered an unethical one as it has a negative impact on the society as a whole.

We need here to understand that the moral background of the decision maker (intrinsic paragon) is the one that will keep her at the end of the day on the good side, but this is not always the case. Very difficult situations and fiscal difficulties might tempt her to decide toward a direction which is 180 degrees different than her own. There were cases, for example, during the last global financial crisis when small business owners who were of a moral stature decided that government was against them as it was posing severe taxation measures which had extremely negative results on the small business operations. In such cases, they felt somehow obliged to decide to evade their tax obligations and to consider such action a moral one as the whole situation, for them, was something like a state of war.

Also, in other situations, like during the pandemic, many small business owners were doing their best to not pay their tax obligations or even not aligned with the restrictions posed by the government in terms of how they needed to operate due to the pandemic because they were on the verge of extinction after several years of crisis and now hit by the pandemic as well. Such difficult times are trying the moral background of all people and in some occasions can be found to be very negative influencers. This is why time and situation that the society is facing can be considered as important parameters that need to be taken under vast consideration in terms of the decision making in small business.

Other parameters that need to be taken under vast consideration as they can be said to be crucial for the decision making are the ethical recognition and the ethical judgment ones (Musbah et al. 2014; 2016). A study conducted in Libya by Musbah et al. (2014; 2016) found that there is significant relationship between ethical recognition and ethical judgment and also between ethical judgment and ethical intention. On the contrary, ethical recognition was not found to be correlated to ethical intention, at least at high extend (Musbah et al. 2014; 2016).

According to a research conducted by Fassin et al. (2011), although small business owners are capable of shaping the corporate culture and enact values other than profit, they also pragmatically and rather clearly tend to differentiate between the various concepts that are related to corporate responsibility and business ethics, while on the contrary somehow they tend to recognize the interrelationships and the interdependencies between such concepts (Fassin et al. 2011). So, although small business owners understand where they are standing in terms of their corporate social responsibility and business ethics, they somehow tend to distance themselves from them. This is extremely important and needs to be investigated further as it gives us another important parameter which can be a strong determinant in terms of decision making in small business: the social distancing of small business owners and the society.

Small business owners, although they know that they are interconnected to the society in which they operate, sometimes do not understand that they are obliged to support this very society via their corporate social responsibility actions and decisions. They tend to not understand the importance for their business to follow such social-focused tactics and actions and they think that by not spending some amount of money toward that direction they are helping their business to go lean. The reality is completely different because life showed us that companies that do not contribute to the society tend to vanish. On the contrary, companies that tend to help people around them not only survive but sustain for long time as the local societies tend to embrace and support them.

Being ethical is a choice and needs to be taken under vast consideration by small business owners. Decision making has so many ethical implications that cannot be taken lightly by the decision makers. Corporate social responsibility is a way of sustainable development for small business owners but also a way of exercising an ethical decision making and acting toward an ethical perspective of business which might have only positive impacts to the society as a whole.

From the above it is clear that small business owners, especially nowadays, need to have, among their skill set, the ability to recognize and deal with complex business ethical issues, as business ethics is always their huge responsibility as they are the decision makers (Bulog and Grancic 2017).

As managers are into decision making day after day, they need to have not only the ability to behave ethically (Bulog and Grancic 2017) and act as a role model, but also the ability to make the right choices under sometimes difficult circumstances and always based on a strong ethical basis.

In this chapter, till now we discussed about the parameters that are involved in the ethical decision-making process. But it can also be said that the ethical decision-making process has four main components which according to Lincoln and Holmes (2011) are:

- Moral sensitivity or moral awareness, which is the individual's ability to understand that the situation in which she is into involves a moral issue that needs to be taken under consideration (Rest 1994, cited in Lincoln and Holmes 2011).
- Moral judgment, which also refers to how we can possibly formulate and evaluate which potential solution that we can offer to the above-mentioned moral issue has a moral justification, or in other words a real one (Rest 1994, cited in Lincoln and Holmes 2011).
- Moral motivation or moral intention, which refers to the intention of the individual to be able to choose the moral one between two or more options; for example, let's imagine a situation in which an individual is facing a dilemma; in other words she has to choose between two options regarding a situation. The number one option will give her money and power and the number two solution will bring her nothing but is the moral one. In this example, the moral motivation is the one that describes the individual's intentions to follow solution number two over number one (Lincoln and Holmes 2011, p. 57).
- Moral courage or moral action, which describes the individual's action when she is involved in a situation that needs to be taken care of with courage, determination, and a sense of following through with the moral decision that took place (Lincoln and Holmes 2011).

So, we can see that many moral aspects are part of an ethical decision-making process and that what makes the difference is the decision maker's moral profile. The decision maker also needs to be consistent and brave as usually ethical decisions can be very difficult as they could find many stakeholders and shareholders against, since their financial prosperity might be damaged.

Of course, one parameter that is important here to be taken under vast consideration is that small businesses, as all business, are being run by people, and people sometimes somehow can feel uncertain in an uncertain environment. Such situations are difficult for business owners who are responsible for the company's survival. When they need to take difficult decisions, in order to be able to stay ethical all the way, they need to have the above-mentioned four components, especially moral courage, because it takes a lot of courage to stay moral and take ethical decisions when the pressure is unprecedented. In such occasions, the commercial and entrepreneurial motivation can be huge and the decision makers might be facing a dilemma, whether to decide ethically or to save their company.

Bulog and Grancic (2017) underline that ethical behavior of the decision makers is of huge strategic importance for their business, as it is one of the most important between different factors that can determine the future of the company in question. This is why the ethical behavior of the decision makers can be considered as one of the key elements that can achieve the company's competitive advantage (Bulog and Grancic 2017), which accordingly can achieve the company's sustainable development on the long run and can bring prosperity to the company and the society.

It is important here to underline the thin red line upon which entrepreneurs many times need to balance. But this fragile equilibrium can be broken in no time if the decision maker has no ethical motivation and has no strong will toward the ethical solution/decision. Ethical and unethical in business sometimes can be seen as a blur line for many, but in fact they are two completely different and distinct areas of life. Business is a part of life and not something out of it. It is something which has an ethical perspective and needs to have one in order to help us create a better world. At the end of the day, everything is about the choices we make as humans, as managers, as CEOs, as leaders. It is up to us to have a positive/ethical impact on not only our business but also the society as a whole.

Ethical Consequences and the Environment

Decision making in both large and small business can have negative implications on many things as we discuss in this chapter. One of the things that is extremely vital and of the greatest importance not only for business but for the whole planet is the environmental impact that they have via their decisions.

In the past years, people all over the world started to realize more and more that in order to be able to face a certain and viable future for us and the generations to come, we need to focus more on how we can start to have a positive impact on the environment which in the past decades was not treated appropriately by organizations, businesses, people, and governments all over the world.

For example, Revell et al. (2009; 2010) stress that what we get from previous studies conducted in the United Kingdom on the environmental practices of small and medium enterprises have depicted that the companies' owners/managers were more or less acting as laggards who try to underplay the environmental impact of their companies' decisions and actions by resisting somehow a more efficient management, from environmental approach, due to its perceived increased cost (Revell et al. 2009; 2010).

The above-mentioned authors stress that this UK reality was not the same several years after, as a recent survey (Revell et al. 2009; 2010) among 220 UK SMEs found that this way of approaching things that we described earlier slowly starts to change toward a more sensitive environmental stance from the part of the SMEs' owners. They add that this is the result of the SMEs' CEOs' change in their perspective as they, slowly, started to realize that it is their responsibility to help the society as a whole to solve specific environmental problems, no matter what the cost is. This is depicted in tougher environmental regulations. It seems that what has motivated small business owners, apart from legislation, was the opportunity for potential cost savings, new customers, and customer retention via the creation of a more environmental friendly business profile which results in a better brand name and higher staff retention, as they are more aligned to the company's mission and vision which above everything else includes an environmental sensitivity (Revell et al. 2009; 2010).

All these concerns have vast impact on how SMEs' owners began thinking, at least in the United Kingdom as the authors indicated, but in general what has happened in the past years is that SME owners, although a bit skeptical regarding the growth potential of an environmental friendly behavior, have started to understand that behind this whole environmental issue there is an opportunity for sustainability and growth (Revell et al. 2009; 2010). They started to understand that their benefit should be aligned with the environmental one.

This alteration on how SMEs' owners perceive their company's position and impact on the environment has a global presence in the past years. It is quite impressive, given the previous decade's approaches, that environmental scanning has become a key factor toward the sustainability of the company's competitive advantage, especially among the SME owners (Analoui and Karami 2002). This is why many consider it as the first and one of the most important steps in the strategic management process as environmental scanning started to be considered as necessary toward the successful alignment of the strategies in question in order to become more competitive toward the achievement of the SMEs' outstanding performance (Analoui and Karami 2002).

It is very important for all small companies to understand that they are operating on our planet as integral parts not only of the society but of the environment as well. This is why they heavily depend on it and on the changes that occur in it (Lekovic et al. 2013). Although they are unable to control the environmental impacts, they need to develop a mechanism which can partially be able to reduce such impacts and in that way to be synchronized with the changes that occur on a global level (Lekovic et al. 2013).

It is important to underline that although such mechanisms might increase the business' operational cost, they will have a strong positive impact on the society as a whole and they will be able to boost profit at the end of each fiscal year. (Lekovic et al. 2013).

It is important here to stress that small business owners one way or another have started understanding that being environmentally sensitive while doing business has a long-term positive impact on both their business and the society in which they operate. Additionally, the cost of such attitude is not that important as what is at stake is much bigger than some earnings of a few businesses. On the other hand, that cost at the end of the day will be more trivial, even from a business perspective, as the result of such actions in terms of branding and customer and employees' retention will be compelling. So, it is more than obvious that small business owner will be benefited in many ways by being environmentally sensitive with their business.

In their research, Caughron et al. (2011) state that environmental factors influence reasoning strategies, reasoning strategies influence sense making, and sense making finally influences ethical decision making. So, we can understand that ethical decision making which has vast environmental implications is based on a chain reaction like the one described in the previous sentence. Small businesses need to highly consider such environmental implications because they operate inside the society which, partially, is their customer base.

How is it possible to expect to sell to a market, part of a society which is devastated due to your decision, for example, to destroy part of a forest in order to build a mall? Although people probably will visit your stores and buy your goods, the negative implications that this decision will have to their well-being will be such that in the long run they will leave you because they will realize that you are not there for them, but that you are there only to serve your commercial and monetary intentions. So, apart from seeing the decision making as an act of strategic and commercial management, small business owners need to see it as an act which has vast ethical implications for both the environment and the society as a whole.

As we discussed briefly in the previous chapter, the open systems theory, accompanied by the stakeholder theory, is a very important parameter that small business owners need to have in mind in order to reach ethical decisions toward the benefit of the environment or the society, as we will see in the next chapter.

In the past, organizations were considered to be closed systems that had no influence from their surrounding environment. This approach has changed during the years and given us the "open systems" theory which is a kind of holistic approach on how the whole system operates. This theory gave us, for the first time, the opportunity to understand that organizations are living things which operate inside an environment (society, markets, the whole world, etc.) and that they interact with it in multiple ways.

As we can see in IAEA's[1] report (2002), within moral philosophy, there are two main theories, namely, "the ethics of ends (utilitarianism)" and the "ethics of duty (deontology)." According to classical utilitarianism, an action is morally correct if it contributes to the general good of human beings to a larger extent than any other possible action (IAEA 2002). So, it is important here to understand that small business owners when they are acting toward a decision making, need to have in mind that for such decision it is good to have a moral base which means that it will benefit the human beings that live on this planet and are part or not of their surrounding society. In fact in our global societies of today's world the effects of small unethical decisions which have negative implications to the society in which small businesses operate or to the environment as a whole might have vast implications in the long run, for the whole planetary eco system.

Author's Notes

In this chapter, we discussed about the decision making in small business and all the parameters that are involved in them.

We also discussed about the ethical consequences that might arise as the result of the decision making in small business and how such consequences might have vast environmental impact.

The following topics need to be discussed:

- The ethical parameters that are involved in the decision-making process of small business management
- The ethical consequences of the decision-making process and how they impact the environment
- Why is it important to take ethical decisions? What impact might such an attitude have in our lives as professionals and society's members?

---

[1] IAEA: International Atomic Energy Agency.

Questions

1. Which are the ethical parameters involved in the decision-making process?
2. Which might be some ethical consequences that arise from the decision-making process in small business?
3. Why and in which ways can the decision-making process have a vast negative environmental impact?

PART II
Company Culture

CHAPTER 4

Company Culture: The Cornerstone of Success

What Do We Mean by the Term "Company Culture"?

Every company has something unique. Although you might be able to find so many companies out there operating in the same industry, in the same niche, and even selling the same products, it is very important to understand that each one of them is unique in a very unique way. And this very unique way is called "company culture."

So, how can we define what company culture is? I found recently a very indicative definition which I give you here:

> Organizational (or company) culture is defined as the underlying beliefs, assumptions, values and ways of interacting that contribute to the unique social and psychological environment of an organization. (Cancialosi 2017)

As we can see from the above definition, two points are the most important, the words "underlying" and "unique." So, the first thing that we can understand is that company culture is not something that is clearly obvious for the people that observe the company from outside because it is something that is underlying. So, we can say that in order to understand it, you need to feel it, live it, and/or interact with the company somehow (e.g., if you are a customer, you can understand that the company in question has a great company culture because during your interaction with the company you will be able to observe how the company's employees feel and react and this fact per se is possible to give you important information regarding the company's culture).

But why company culture so important? Is it something that can really make a difference for any company? Is it something so strong?

According to (Levine 2018; 2019), company culture is really critical for all companies. In fact, it can be considered as a top driver of fiscal performance among other equally important things.

But is culture something that each company explicitly states and runs? The answer, according to James et al. (2019), is "no." Company culture is rather implicit; also it can be said that it is rather emotional than rational and this implicit way of being expressed is the one that makes it not so easy to work with, but on the other hand is exactly why it is so powerful. According to the same author (James et al. 2019), each company culture is based upon three elements as seen in Table 4.1.

Table 4.1 The three elements of company culture (James et al. 2019)

THE THREE ELEMENTS OF COMPANY CULTURE
"Traits, characteristics that are at the heart of people's emotional connection to what they do"
"Keystone behaviors, actions that would lead your company to succeed if they were replicated at a greater scale"
"Authentic informal leaders, people who have a high degree of 'emotional intuition' or social connectedness"

As we can see from the table these three elements are vital and very important and as such they can play a critical role in the company's overall performance. As James et al. (2019) underline, the leverage of such elements can play the role of a catalyst inside the company via the positive change they can bring as people will feel to be committed in the company's new, for example, initiatives not only in a rational way, but also and foremost in an emotional one. This emotional parameter is the one that at the end of the day will make the difference and will be able to elicit enthusiasm and creativity, things that will build the kind of powerful company that people recognize for its unique value and effectiveness (James et al. 2019).

So, company culture is this implicit part of the company that has a huge positive or negative effect on people's behavior, engagement, feelings, way of working and living, and this very thing is the one that makes it, as we saw in the previous paragraph, a real catalyst for the company's overall performance.

Kucharska and Kowalczyk (2019) correctly stated, in their survey regarding the connecting links between company culture, performance, CSR and reputation, that "The people are the company."

Jain and Jain (2013) state that the company culture is composed of several factors like:

- Values
- Norms
- Tangible signs (artifacts) of organization members
- Leadership

All these factors can be seen as elements that exist inside a company culture and are unique parts of it.

This is a very important statement because it gives in just a few words the gist of what business is all about or at least what business should be about. It is important to understand that business should not only be about the money. If this is the approach, many problems will arise in both short and long terms. The right company culture will be able, if implemented, to establish a human-centric approach which will have people in the epicenter of the business itself, something which will create for the business the competitive advantage needed in order to excel. The reason is simple because a great human-centric company culture will be able to engage employees in a greater way and will make them do the extra mile when needed plus it will be able to make them excel in what they do as the way they will be treated is always depicted in their behavior toward customers. And if this behavior is great, then customer retention will increase and with it ROI will increase as well. This fact per se is a vivid depiction of why the right company culture is so important for every company out there.

The Role of Company Culture in the Company's Performance

As we saw in the previous chapter, company culture is a very powerful "tool" in the hands of every company. It is that weapon that, if properly utilized, will make a difference for the company in question and for the lives of the people who are working for this company as well.

In terms of performance, company culture is a very critical element of the overall company's existence. As Papke (2013) stresses, companies live and die based on their ability to communicate with their customers in order to listen to their needs but, more importantly, by their ability to be in alignment with the promises that their brand makes to them. What is important is that this alignment can only be achieved by a leadership that defines the companies' vision and strategies in a concise and clear way in terms of roles, expectations, and goals of all team members of the organization. In that way, customers' expectations will be clearly defined and the brand will be remembered by the customers as the one that brings solutions to their problems, something which in the long run will increase customer retention and of course ROI, not to mention that it will also build a solid brand name for the company in question via word of mouth in physical and digital form (Papke 2013).

In order to achieve that goal, companies need to create and implement a company culture which will have everyone aligned to this vision and will make everyone understand that they need to be aligned and responsible for following the brand promise to the company's customers (Papke 2013). The company's environment which can be translated as the company's culture will be the means toward such alignment and the one that will guarantee that employees will be determined to live up to customers' expectations by following the company's promise to them.

We all know that in an ever-changing world as the one in which we are living, being innovative is extremely important as it will help you acquire the competitive advantage needed and meet your customers' expectations and live by the brand's promise. As innovation is so important, it is obvious that it is something that companies need to pursue with huge commitment.

According to Kratzer et al. (2017), innovation is driven by the people who form the heart of the company's innovation activities. So, it is very important that the people who are involved in the innovation process inside the company will not face impediments during their efforts. This is why it is imperative that a company culture that favors innovation should be implemented in the company in question. This innovation culture will help people to implement their innovative ideas in the right way without facing problems or obstacles that will hinder their way. So, having an innovative spirit embedded inside the company's culture is something that is very important and can have vast impact on the company's overall performance.

As we saw in Table 4.1, company culture is, above many other things, about people's lives. So, if people feel satisfied with their working environment and working roles, they will be able to excel and do the extra mile that will make them more committed and productive, something that will help the company's overall performance to a huge degree.

For people working in a specific company to be able to feel well in their working environment, it is very important to be able to feel safe and healthy. Especially nowadays during the pandemic that Covid-19 caused, it is imperative for people to feel that they work in an environment that will not jeopardize their health and safety. Fabius et al. (2013) stress that implementing cultures that are focused on health and safety is something that will give to such companies the competitive advantage that they are seeking for and they will be able to yield greater value to their investors. This is extremely important and can be achieved because employees who feel that they are operating in an environment of safety, and that, above everything else, will keep them healthy as well, can focus on their jobs and be more productive.

A very interesting read is the one of Jain and Jain (2013), which stress that knowledge management[1] and company culture need to be combined in a way that they can together direct day-to-day behavior, support structural changes and processes, and create the climate needed in order to successfully support the implementation of innovation strategy, a strategy that will bring more value to both the company and its customers. Jain and Jain (2013) also underline the importance of company culture as the steering wheel toward the increase of the employees' productivity

---

[1] Knowledge management: "Knowledge management is the systematic management of an organization's knowledge assets for the purpose of creating value and meeting tactical & strategic requirements; it consists of the initiatives, processes, strategies, and systems that sustain and enhance the storage, assessment, sharing, refinement, and creation of knowledge" (knowledge-management-tools.net 2018).

and of course the company's performance levels, two parameters that will definitely increase ROI.

Atafar et al. (2013) in their study concluded that several different components of company culture are correlated with productivity. These components are creativity, accepting risk, support, integration, control, identification, communication, and reward policies. Such elements are critical components of company culture and can increase productivity in several ways as they can solve many problems that arise throughout the company's life and can implement excellence and bring value to customers.

The environment that the company creates affects the employees' well-being and this in turn influences their effectiveness toward their goals and the company's goals (Clements-Croome 2015). Poor environments, and thus company culture, increase absenteeism and decrease performance. Clements-Croome (2015) also stresses that high-quality environmental design can be seen as a long-term investment, as people tend to be healthier, while staff retention increases and productivity becomes higher as well. Building better workspaces can be seen as part of a great company culture which increase morale and make people feel better, which makes them much more effective on their daily job runtime.

Another way that company culture uses to increase productivity is via the implementation of tactics that are embedded in the very company culture and that are focused in increasing presenteeism, which is a growing problem in developed countries (Ammendolia et al. 2016). People that work inside a nonhealthy company culture tend to have increased mental health problems, something which not only increase absenteeism, but also reduce performance and productivity. Depression and stress, as results of a bad company culture, are factors that create a huge problem to the companies in question (Ammendolia et al. 2016). It is remarkable that, as Ammendolia et al. (2016) stress, the economic costs that are related to presenteeism exceed those that are related to absenteeism and employer health costs as well. This is why in several companies operating in the developed countries, employers are implementing workplace health promotion and wellness programs to improve the health among their workforce and reduce absenteeism (Ammendolia et al. 2016). Such problem can create huge negative impact on productivity and, of course, ROI.

Another paragon that is preventive of productivity as it creates a lot of problems not only inside of the company but also in the company's brand name and customer retention is integrity. As Bussmann and Anja (2019) stress, this is something that requires a tone from the top. As we discussed earlier, company culture is something that comes from the top. The company's CEO is the one who implements the specific culture and this is why she is also responsible for implementing a culture of integrity and ethical values. This is something that requires her exercising an ethical leadership.[2] Preventing crime is something that in the long run will increase productivity as it will give to the people outside the company the picture of a healthy and trusted company. Never forget that in business, being trusted is the alpha and the omega.

But for a company to prevent crime and to exercise successfully an ethical leadership it should be able to implement a company culture that promotes integrity and ethical decision making. This culture needs to be based on open communication, transparency, and compliance with the rules and rejection of people who are behaving based on their own interest only (Bussmann and Anja 2019). Such transparency and ethical basis are extremely important company culture components that can be reflected in an increased ROI in the long run and in building an impressive and trustworthy brand name that will increase customer retention as well.

Management Control Systems and Company Culture

A very important part of management includes the so-called "management control systems" (MCSs). They are devices or systems which become operational via the use of resources, like humans and financial resources and which are used in order to ensure that the objectives that the company posed from the beginning are carried out in the best possible way and toward growth and increased ROI by controlling, encouraging, enabling or, sometimes, even forcing employees in order to make them perform according to these company objectives (Merchant & V.D.Stede 2012, cited in Karaoulanis 2015).

---

[2] Ethical leadership: According to Blackman (2018), "ethical leadership means acting according to your moral principles in your day-to-day business life and decision-making. To put it simply, it means doing the right thing."

MCSs can be seen as a communicating language which is implemented by the higher hierarchy of the company throughout the organization and which creates a unifying way of thinking throughout the personnel of all levels and helps the organization to manage the potential interdependencies that arise between several parts of the organization. It can also be seen as the means used in order to help the organization to evolve and also to make the planned organizational changes possible via several ways/methods that might be used (Chenhall and Euske 2007, cited in Karaoulanis 2015).

They consist of four main categories of controls, which we can see in Table 4.2:

- Results controls
- Action controls
- Personnel controls
- Cultural controls (Merchant & V.D.Stede 2012, cited in Karaoulanis 2015).

Results controls are the controls that motivate employees in an indirect way, with a kind of reward (Merchant & V.D.Stede 2012, pp. 29–40, cited in Karaoulanis 2015).

Table 4.2 Management control systems' main categories (Merchant & V.D.Stede 2012, cited in Karaoulanis 2015)

Management Control Systems' Categories
Results controls
Action controls
Personnel controls
Cultural controls

Actions controls are controls that have a more direct way of interacting. They motivate employees in a direct way, by taking certain steps that ensure the right actions of the employees (Merchant & V.D.Stede 2012, pp. 81, 88, cited in Karaoulanis 2015)

Personnel controls ensure that employees will control and motivate themselves by introducing specific behaviors which make them act in alignment with the interests of the organization way (Merchant & V.D.Stede 2012, pp. 81, 88, cited in Karaoulanis 2015).

Cultural controls encourage employees to monitor and influence each other through a specific cultural framework that is implemented in the organization (Merchant & V.D.Stede 2012, pp. 81, 88, cited in Karaoulanis 2015).

The implementation of such MCSs can only be done successfully if there is a good understanding from the personnel part of the company's objectives and strategy, as the people who will be responsible for their design and implementation will be part of the company's personnel that are assigned with this role (Merchant & V.D.Stede 2012, p. 209, cited in Karaoulanis 2015).

The use of MCSs should present an interactive nature, in order to be able to achieve communication between managers and employees of all levels of hierarchy. In this way, it can be possible to debate or even challenge the underlying assumptions and action plans that drive an organization's activities. What is interesting to mention here is that both employees and managers who attained different sets of information can come together and, by the combination of their knowledge, be more productive in terms of achieving organization goals. This is the recipe of success in terms of the company's inner communication and execution and it is something that can successfully be achieved via the right use of the right MCSs (Abernethy and Lillis 1995: Spekle 2001, cited in Karaoulanis 2015). This interactive use of MCSs is of utmost importance for organizations who are seeking the opportunity to communicate, execute, and learn throughout the organization (Henri 2006, p. 533, cited in Karaoulanis 2015).

Another important mission that MCSs have is to help the company in question to implement in the most successful possible way its strategic vision. So, it is easy to say that the use of MCSs has also a very important role as an important part of the company's strategy implementation[3] (Henri 2006, p. 548, cited in Karaoulanis 2015).

---

[3] *Strategy implementation:* With the term "strategy implementation" we mean the managerial activity by which the chosen strategy is being translated into actions (Johnson and Scholes 1989, cited in Langfield-Smith 1997, p. 210, cited in Karaoulanis 2015).

Finally another important point that we want to stress is that MCSs are critical when they are used in companies which implement the so-called "management by expectation"[4] approach as Merchant and Stede in "Management Control Systems" indicate (2012, p. 32, cited in Karaoulanis 2015).

As we saw in the earlier paragraphs, MCSs are playing a vital role in many organizational activities, like communication, strategy, and controlling. A very important role that they are also playing is in terms of their correlation with the company's culture. As they are used by the upper management as the means of communicating and implementing various company policies and ideas they need to be used upon a company culture that is defined or that it defines (both ways actually work) toward their common goal, the implementation of the operations management, including strategy implementation.

According to Reginato and Guerreiro (2013), there is a significant relationship between the "construction" of the organizational culture and the MCSs that the specific company is using, something that signals that the organizational culture has a very strong influence in terms of choosing the right MCSs (Reginato and Guerreiro 2013).

Not all MCSs are suitable for all companies. Their suitability has to do with many parameters that need to be investigated. Company culture is one of them, so you cannot use any kind of control systems in all kinds of company cultures without thinking. For example, the chances to have a successful personnel control system implemented in a company which has, for example, a flat hierarchy culture are likely small. This is why company culture plays a crucial role in terms of choosing the right MCSs. In simple words, the process can be depicted in Figure 4.1.

MCS can be related to company culture in multiple ways. For example, empowerment, as managerial practice that springs via company culture can be positively related to innovation capability for small and medium enterprices (SMEs) (Çakar and Ertürk 2010).

---

[4] *Management by expectation:* Managers also have the tendency to investigate and intervene in several ways when they think that their subordinates' performance is deviating from the set targets (Merchant & V.D. Stede 2012, p. 32, cited in Karaoulanis 2015).

| CEO | ⟹ | COMPANY CULTURE | ⟹ | MCSs |

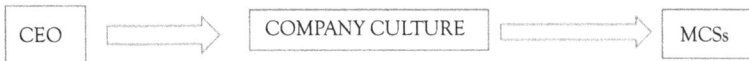

Figure 4.1 *The way of implementing MCSs*

On the other hand, while the right company culture tends to make employees more creative and innovative, the company needs a special control that will be related to the very company culture that the company decided to implement, such as personnel control.

This is because, for example, the company might need to implement such controls in order to be able to hire the right personnel in terms of who is really suitable for the specific company culture that is implemented. Personnel controls are the right instruments in such case because they can help the company very much in terms of recruiting, training, and so on (Efferin and Hopper 2007). What is very important here is that the specific company culture has already a human-centric approach which empowers employees, for example, via training because personnel control takes care more about recruitment and training of the employees.

An important way via which MCSs are correlated with company culture is when, via the use of informal control systems such as group behavior, organizational norms, and organizational beliefs, companies can implement ethical work climates or in other words ethical company culture. Such cultures are based on mutual trust between the company's employees. Such ethical contact can therefore be implemented via the organizational culture which has a strong ethical direction and can be "controlled" via the use of such informal MCSs (Goebel et al. 2017). In this example, company culture and MCSs are interconnected and one supports the other in a coherent way toward the materialization of the CEO's mentality and perspectives of what is ethical on a company level.

Sawade and Tobita (2009) found that there can be several combinations of MCSs that can affect employees' motivation and, in the long run, organization's performance, and that such combinations differ according to the specific organizational culture type. For example, organizations that have implemented more flexible culture are more likely to have social control[5] and belief control, while on the other hand, organizations with control culture are more likely to have accounting controls[6] and so on (Sawabe and Tobita 2009).

Here we need to add that in terms of implementation controls,[7] one can argue that if MCSs are implemented in an environment which can be characterized as an uncertain one, then it is very likely that we need to use a combination of both formal (e.g., tight financial controls) and informal (e.g., flexible, interpersonal interactions) management controls (Chenhall 2003, cited in Eldridge et al. 2014; p. 68, cited in Karaoulanis 2015).

We need here to bear in mind that uncertainty has some potent effects on MCSs, such as the difficulty in implementing action controls (Merchant & V.D. Stede 2012, p. 686, cited in Karaoulanis 2015).

So, we can understand from the above that uncertainty, for example, is a situation which can have vast influence on the implementation of the company culture since it will interfere with the CEO's mentality and her risk-averse or not perception of things, something which has to do also with the person's social characteristics. Under this prism, the types of MCSs that the company will be using in such an unstable environment will be different than the ones that would have been used if the situation was smoother and the company culture was a different one.

Another way of implementing the specific MCSs that can be seen as the result of the implementation of a specific company culture is the case

---

[5] *Social controls*: "the rules and standards of society that circumscribe individual action through the inculcation of conventional sanctions and the imposition of formalized mechanisms" (Merriam-webster.com n.d.).

[6] *Accounting controls*: "Accounting controls are the procedures and the methods which are applied by an entity for the assurance, validity and accuracy of the financial statements but these accounting controls are applied for compliance and as a safeguard for the company and not to comply with the laws, rules and the regulations" (wallstreetmojo.com n.d.).

[7] *Implementation controls*: "Management efforts designed to assess whether the overall strategy should be changed in light of results associated with the incremental actions that implemented the overall strategy. These are usually associated with specific strategic thrusts or projects and with predetermined milestone reviews" (the-definition.com n.d.).

of incentives. Incentives are a crucial paragon in the design of a complete and effective MCS. We can also refer to them as "performance-dependent" rewards. Their role is to be able to provide employees the impetus is needed in order to be aligned with the organization's objectives (Merchant & V.D. Stede 2012, p. 368, cited in Karaoulanis 2015).

It is important to notice here that there are several purposes that the incentives serve, such as to inform employees of the performance area in which they need to focus, to motivate them toward a better overall performance, to attract and retain high-quality employees, and to serve non-control purposes like correlating compensation with firm performance (Merchant & V.D. Stede 2012, pp. 368–69, cited in Karaoulanis 2015).

Incentives are a very important part of company culture as they show the employees a clear path via which, by achieving their goals, they can get a better income, a promotion, and so on. What is important here is that we need to understand that although incentives are MCSs that ensure the employees' overall focus on targets that were set by, for example, the CEO of the company, the underlying company culture is the one that permits the implementation of such incentives as MCSs. A culture that wants to reward the employees that work hard and that are persistent toward the company goals is a culture that has a human-centric approach and that values its work force.

So, it is obvious from the above that the right company culture is the one that tells us which MCSs we need to use in order to be aligned with it.

Finally, another example of these interconnections between the company culture and the MCSs is that when, for example, we have a high organizational error management culture, which means a culture that conceptualized to include norms and common practices in organizations like communicating about errors, detecting, analyzing, and correcting errors as quickly as possible, we are apt to make a huge step toward the reduction of negative and the promotion of positive error consequences (Van Dyck et al. 2005). In such cultures we need to implement, for example, results management systems that will be able to monitor the results of the processes that take place in the company.

The correlation between the company culture and the implementation of the right MCSs is obvious from the above. Company culture can be seen as the platform upon which we can implement the suitable MCSs that will serve with excellence the specific company culture. The CEO's mentality though is very important as well as it is the one which is responsible in the first place for the implementation of the specific company culture. The MCSs, as mechanisms that are responsible for monitoring the right execution of all projects and the overall organizational performance, are the levers via which a company with an ethical background will be able to ensure ethical operations. This fact per se is extremely important if we can understand that the company's brand name and its overall existence are based upon this very ethical operation which will increase, above so many other things like employees' retention, the bond of trust between the company and its customers' potential and will also have a very positive impact on the company's brand name.

The Role of Leadership in Company Culture Implementation

In the previous chapters we discussed about the importance of the implementation of the right company culture for the company in question. We also saw the correlation between company culture and profitability and how we can use the MCSs needed in order to implement the right company culture and run our organization smoothly. In this section, we will discuss about the correlation between leadership and company culture and how this correlation can affect positively the implementation of such culture.

Effective leadership correlates to great company culture, something which looks very natural as leadership has to do, as we saw earlier, with influence and authority. Since this is the case it is easy to understand that leaders can reinforce the values needed in order to implement a great company culture. This is why the different leadership styles or whether leadership will be effective or not are parameters that can influence the implementation of the company's culture (octanner.com n.d.).

According to SHRM (cited in octanner.com n.d.),[8] leaders need to be deliberate in creating a great company culture, a company culture that will facilitate employees to become better and thrive (octanner.com n.d.).

---

[8] SHRM: Society for Human Resource Management.

Leadership is a very important part of all business and is the substance that makes the difference in every business, and its impact on all parts of every business is huge.

A great definition of what is leadership is the following: "leadership is the ability to inspire confidence and support among the people who are needed to achieve organizational goals" (Durbin 2010). From that definition we can see that the main keywords are "inspire confidence and support." So, leadership is about inspiration. It is about someone inspiring her people toward a common goal. A very important point in terms of leadership is its difference to management. In order to understand the unique substance of leadership we first need to take a look at what management is about.

So, management is about planning, organizing, directing, or leading people, controlling them (Durbin 2010). Having these managerial functions in mind we can understand that leadership is about dealing with the interpersonal aspects of a manager's job such as change, inspiration, motivation, and influence (Dubrin 2010).

So, we can see from the above that a manager is a rather rational guy who is dealing with structured tasks of everyday business life. On the other hand, the leader has a more human-centric approach in business.

In Table 4.3 we can see the main differences between the characteristics of a manager and a leader:

This table is indicative of the difference between the leader and the manager. It is obvious that the leader is the one who embraces the human nature in the workplaces and tries to make a difference by creating a great climate inside the job and by harvesting people's efforts in a more "humanitarian" way via paths like loyalty, being part of the team, and feeling valued. It's all about doing the right things and doing the things right as a manager perceives them.

But being a leader is not something easy. One of the main leadership components is the enthusiasm and the ability to work with people (Dubrin 2010). Leadership is a sum of actions that at the end of the day will be able to not only affect positively the personalities and the abilities of the workers but also, via such affection, increase the company's performance.

A leader is someone who, as we saw, can influence people around her. So influencing positively an employee in a job context is vital. But are all

Table 4.3 Leaders versus managers (Dubrin 2010, p. 5)

Leader	Manager
Visionary	Rational
Passionate	Business-like
Creative	Persistent
Inspiring	Tough minded
Innovative	Analytical
Courageous	Structured
Imaginative	Deliberative
Experimental	Authoritative
Independent	Stabilizing
Shares knowledge	Centralizes knowledge
Trusting	Guarded
Warm and radiant	Cool and reserved
Expresses humility	Rarely admits to be wrong
Initiator	Implementer
Acts like a coach, consultant, teacher	Acts as a boss
Does the right things	Does things right
Inspires through great ideas	Commands through position
Knows that results are achieved through people	Focuses on results

employees getting influenced to the same degree? In fact there are several kinds of followers among the employees that work in any company. They are the isolates, the bystanders, the participants, the activists, and the diehards (Durbin 2010).

Isolates are completely detached and passively accept the company's status quo by not taking any kind of action to bring about changes (Durbin 2010).

Bystanders can be seen as "free riders" who are basically detached when the situation fits their personal interests and ambitions (Dubrin 2010).

Participants are the ones that show enough engagement to invest their own time, for example, to learn new technology via a seminar, in order to make a difference (Dubrin 2010).

Activists are heavily engaged and they are eager to demonstrate their support or opposition (Dubrin 2010).

Diehards are the ones that are very engaged to the point that they are willing to go down for their own cause or even willing to oust their own leader if they feel that she is heading toward the wrong direction in business and life (Durbin 2010).

All these categories of followers/employees show a different degree of engagement and this is why leadership needs to address to them in different ways in order to get the best out of each category.

Of course leaders need, above everything, to lead by example in order to be able to inspire their followers—to be role models. It is very important to "walk the talk" otherwise they will not be able to convince anyone about anything at all.

Another important point regarding leadership is that there is not just one leadership style. We have many. The most important ones are the following:

1. *Transactional Leadership*: It is a "I give you this and you do that in return" style; to put it simply this kind of leaders give instructions and then they announce rewards and penalties according to the outcome of their efforts (Boogaard n.d.).
2. *Transformational Leadership*: It is a style which aims to change the business or the group that they lead by inspiring their employees to innovate (Boogaard n.d.).
3. *Servant Leadership*: This is the most human-centric approach of leadership. Servant leaders are the ones who are not into trying to inspire people toward following their lead. They are mostly and above everything into channeling the majority of their energy into finding ways to help their followers. In simple words, they prioritize the other people's needs above their own. It's a nonselfish approach of leadership (Boogaard n.d.).
4. *Democratic or Participative Leadership*: This kind of leadership is the one which tries to involve all employees in the decision-making process one way or the other. It instills a more democratic perspective in business. Leaders of this kind value the input of others and encourage it (Boogaard n.d.).
5. *Autocratic Leadership*: Autocratic leaders are the ones that follow the motto "my way or the highway." They are the ones that see themselves

as having absolute power over their employees and as such they can make decisions on behalf of their subordinates. They dictate not only what needs to be done but also how these tasks should be completed. It's a way of micromanagement[9] in some sense (Boogaard n.d.).

6. *Bureaucratic Leadership*: This is the kind of leadership that "goes by the book." In other words these leaders follow a prescribed set of boxes to check in order to be considered as accomplishers. They have a so-called "hierarchical authority" which means that their power comes mainly via their formal position or title and not from their unique traits and characteristics that they have. To put it even more simply, they make people listen to them without inspiring them (Boogaard n.d.).

7. *Laissez Faire Leadership*: This kind of leaders provides their followers all the needed tools and resources in order to help them accomplish their job. When they do that they don't start micromanaging but rather they stay back and let the team do their moves, take their decisions, and get the job done. It can be said that they follow an approach that is the opposite of micromanagement (Boogaard n.d.).

8. *Charismatic Leadership*: These leaders are people who have charisma. They are people who have magnetic personalities and they follow a path which is mainly about encouraging behaviors through strict instructions. They use eloquent communication and persuasion in order to unite their team toward a common goal. They have the charisma to lay out their vision in such a vivid and persuading way that they can easily make their followers excited about that common goal (Boogaard n.d.).

All these different leadership styles are in simple words ways of making the job done via approaches that in some occasions are quite human centric like with the servant leader style.

The job of a great leader is not only about doing the job; it is more about influencing positively her followers in a way that she can have a positive impact not only on their professional lives but on their lives as a

---

[9] Micromanager: "A person who is driven by fear and anxiety into meddling with others' work. Micromanagers are bosses or peers" (urbandictionary.com n.d.).

whole. Via this kind of leadership, people are happy, they see their efforts to be rewarded, and they see themselves getting improved in terms of their professional acumen. In addition, since they feel happy, they return back home happy with a positive attitude and more confidence and in that way they can become better partners in life, brothers and sisters, friends, and finally citizens. So, we can understand that this kind of great leadership is a leadership which has a huge social responsibility as well.

In order for leaders to be able to reach and influence their audience which of course is the company's employees, they need to use a specific "platform" which is called company culture.

Via the use of a great company culture, great leadership can be implemented and can make a difference.

According to a research conducted by Rogers (2017), organizations by giving to their employees opportunities to participate on cross-functional teams, to learn new skills, to provide input, to expand responsibilities, and to get exposure to other business functions regardless of their actual title and position are the ones that do better. This kind of companies exercises specific leadership styles like "laissez faire," "democratic," and "servant" leadership. Via this kind of leadership they can implement a great company culture with a human-centric approach which values employees and makes them happy in their working environment.

According to Lanthier (2016), company culture can vastly influence the company's productivity, customer satisfaction, and of course retention, team buy-in, and happiness, thus ROI in both the short and long runs. Employee retention, which is another important factor in team building toward high results, can come via encouraging innovation. In this scenario which can be said to be ideal and can lead to increased ROI without doubt, the company's executives play a vital role as long as they are leading by example (Lanthier 2016). Leading by example, or being a "role model," is a part of leadership which is crucial for companies that need to implement the right company culture. Servant leaders who are willing to put their priorities aside for their followers' common good need are the ones that are going to implement a company culture that is all about the team and the common goal. But in order for such goals to be achieved the real leader needs to lead by example. You cannot preach one thing and the other. If you do that it is impossible to be able to cultivate the right spirit inside your team and of course you cannot implement a great company culture as well.

Another study that was conducted by Widodo and Silitonga (2017) among 2,844 employees in six retail companies across Indonesia determined that the paragons that have significant influence on company performance either partially or simultaneously are the leadership style, the company culture, and the human resource development. What we see here is that leadership style is crucial in terms of company performance. So, as company performance is connected via strong bonds with the company culture, we can understand that company performance is also strongly connected with the leadership style that it is exercised by the company owner and which is responsible for the overall company culture implementation as well.

The above assumption becomes a certainty if we could take a thorough look into any small business. The leadership style is crucial and dictates the company culture of any small businesses. As the CEO of the company with the way she leads is responsible for the implementation of the company culture, her leadership style is the one that poses the rules that govern this very company culture. This fact per se has huge influence on how employees feel and react and in the long run it will also affect how these very employees treat the company's customers and this is a decisive factor in terms of ROI and customer retention.

Another important paragon that needs to be taken into consideration when we try to examine how leadership styles influence the implementation of the right company culture is the culture of the employees per se. Kuchinke (1999) conducted a survey between two companies, a U.S. one and a German one in the telecommunication industry.

By the use of two theories that are well known, Avolio's (1991) "full range leadership theory"[10] and Hofstede's (1980) "theory of

---

[10] Full range leadership theory (FRLT): "the FRLT denotes three typologies of leadership behavior: transformational, transactional, and non-transactional laissez-faire leadership, which are represented by nine distinct factors. The most widely used survey instrument to assess these nine factors in the FRLT has been the Multifactor Leadership Questionnaire (MLQ) Hunt 1999, Lowe et al. 1996, Yukl 1999" (Antonakis, Avolio, and Sivasubramaniam 2003).

culture,"[11] he came to the conclusion that there were lower levels of transformational leadership among the German workers but no differences in leadership styles between different job categories in both countries. The explanation came from differences in company culture, on country level, between the employees in the two companies (Kuchinke 1999). This result shows that although the company culture is strongly correlated with the leadership style that is used in order for this very company culture to be implemented, other paragons are vital as well and needed to be taken under consideration by the leader like the cultural background of the employees. In large multinationals this is a must, but in small and medium enterprises, although this needs to be taken under strong consideration as we live in a global society with people from different socioeconomic backgrounds, it is not that profound.

It is clear that leadership plays a vital role not only in company culture implementation but also in the choice of which company culture should be implemented in a specific company. It has to do with the CEO's mentality and of course with the CEO's leadership style which can be seen as part of her mentality as well. A research conducted by Gholamzadeh et al. (2014) showed that transformational and transactional leadership styles can influence vastly and positively the organizational culture, while on the other hand, laissez faire leadership style can only have a negative one.

Of course, this can be the basis of a huge debate. Are the specific leadership styles the ones that really and always have this kind of influence in every company's culture? Is this specific company in which this research took place just one of the millions out there that these specific leadership styles had such influence? In other words, is this research an indicative one upon which we should be based?

---

[11] Theory of culture: "Hofstede's Cultural Dimensions Theory, developed by Geert Hofstede, is a framework used to understand the differences in culture across countries and to discern the ways that business is done across different cultures. In other words, the framework is used to distinguish between different national cultures, the dimensions of culture, and assess their impact on a business setting" (corporatefinanceinstitute.org n.d.).

It is the author's prevalent opinion that each company has a different "DNA." And by the term DNA here we mean that each company has those specific characteristics that are unique and can be held as responsible, at least to some degree, for the results that a specific leadership style has on its culture. Different companies consist of different people with different cultural, ethnical, personal characteristics. Also different CEOs that implement the same leadership style might have different results as paragons like their gender, background, and life philosophy, which might make a difference in terms of how this specific leadership style is implemented in the specific company. As we saw earlier, cultural characteristics are an important paragon that gets involved in company culture implementation and therefore needs to be taken under vast consideration.

Another important factor that can be seen as part of the overall company culture is the so-called "quality culture."[12] Quality culture is a part of the overall company culture and has vast impact on the company's performance as it can be the lever via which personnel work can be improved via a day-to-day procedure. This procedure, according to Baravska (2016; 2015), is based upon two pillars, the company culture and the leadership of the company in question. In fact, quality can be said to be based on cultural perspectives that are adapted by the specific company, or as we said earlier, are part of the company's "DNA." So, as Baravska (2016; 2015) stresses, quality is implemented not only via the use of specific tools and methods but it can be seen as the result of cultural factors, exactly the company's values and practices, which, to add, are embedded deep into the company's culture.

Baravska (2016; 2015), concludes that both the company's leadership style and culture are of pinnacle importance and are the main pillars upon which the development and implementation of the company's quality culture, always as integral part of the company's culture, are based. The strong bond that exists between leadership and empowerment of the personnel toward the implementation of a quality culture are the main responsible factors for the robust implementation of it (Baravska 2015; 2016).

---

[12] Quality culture: "A true quality culture is an environment where team members genuinely care about the quality of their work, and make decisions based on achieving that level of quality" (Speer 2019).

From the above it is obvious that leadership and company culture are going hand in hand in every company. In fact, leadership can be seen as the means that are used in order to reach the implementation of the company culture itself.

Author's Notes

In this chapter, the main topic of discussion was the company culture. We started by analyzing what we mean by the term "company culture" and its main characteristics. We continued by stressing the three elements of company culture and the role that company culture plays in the company's overall performance.

Continually, we discussed about the MCSs and the correlation between them and the company culture. Finally, we stressed the role of leadership in company culture implementation.

The following topics need to be discussed:

- What is company culture?
- What are the main elements of company culture?
- The role of company culture in the company's overall performance
- What do we mean by the term "management control systems" and what is their role in company culture implementation?
- What do we mean by the term "leadership"? What are the main leadership styles and how do they impact the company culture implementation?

Questions

1. What is the definition of "company culture"?
2. Which are the main elements/characteristics of a company culture?
3. Which is the role that company culture plays in the company's overall performance?
4. What do we mean by the term "management control systems"?
5. What is the interconnection between management control systems and company culture?
6. What do we mean by the term leadership?
7. What are the differences between management and leadership?
8. What is the role of leadership in company culture implementation?

CHAPTER 5

Company Culture in Small Business

Small Business and Company Culture: A Strong Bond

Company culture is an integral part of every company as we saw in the previous chapter. As small businesses are companies as well, company culture is an important part of their entities as well. In fact it is a huge part of them and has to do a lot with the company's overall performance and day-to-day activities.

As we discussed in Chapter 2, small businesses are a very important part of each society inside which they operate. They are the backbone of each society and therefore it is important that they operate smoothly because otherwise huge problems will arise mainly on societal level.

As such, small businesses, which are mainly family owned, need to understand the importance of company culture in their operations as well as the role of leadership that comes for the above (from the CEO, the owner of the company), not only as the means for the implementation of a functional company culture but as an overall catalyst in their operations.

A very important factor, especially in the contemporary world, is sustainability.[1] Sustainability can be achieved via the right methods and initiative that spring from the company's CEO and implemented via her leadership inside the company's DNA which is the company's

---

[1] Sustainability: "Sustainability focuses on meeting the needs of the present without compromising the ability of future generations to meet their needs. The concept of sustainability is composed of three pillars: economic, environmental, and social—also known informally as profits, planet, and people" (Investopedia (2) n.d.).

culture. This fact per se is of huge importance not only in big but also in small companies as it can be seen as part of their corporate social responsibility (CSR).[2]

CSR is also an integral part of the company's culture and needs to be implemented by the owner of the small business and to become part of the employees' mentality as well as they need to understand that they need to contribute toward a better society.

Another factor that needs to be integral part of small businesses' company culture is the business' corporate sustainability (CS).[3]

Recent research on small business indicated that CS activities have been developed in isolation and not as part of the companies' culture via the companies' business activities (Witjes et al. 2017).

Both CSR and CS are important factors for small business, whether they can be seen via the prism of the open systems theory, which indicates that all businesses are integral part of the societies in which they operate and as such are in constant two-way communication and exchange with them, or via the business growth one. The implementation of both CSR and CS activities as part of the company's overall culture, apart from creating only positive results for the society as a whole, will also increase the company's growth via its sustainable development, the brand awareness, and the customer retention that will be achieved in the long run.

---

[2] Corporate social responsibility (CSR): an organization's responsibility for the impacts of its activities on the society and the environment, that is, through transparent and ethical behavior that:
- Contributes to sustainable development, including health and the welfare of society,
- Takes into account the expectations of stakeholders,
- Is in compliance with applicable law and consistent with international norms of behavior, and
- Is integrated throughout the organization and implemented in its relations.
  (Ecovadis.com n.d.)

[3] Corporate sustainability: "A business approach that creates long-term shareholder value by embracing opportunities and managing risks deriving from economic, environmental and social developments" (Guides.library.Yale.edu n.d.).

If both factors are seen as parts of small business' company culture they can easily make us understand the importance of company culture for small business.

Another important factor that needs to be stressed regarding the importance and the impact of company culture in small business is that company culture is a huge influence on the small business knowledge management processes. What is also important here to underline is that small businesses usually suffer from the lack of resources both human and financial. This is why is not easy to implement such procedures, although it is sometimes imperative to develop advanced knowledge management systems and embed them in their company culture (Prystupa-Rządca 2017).

Disseminating and using knowledge throughout the company is critical because in that way the human resources of the company can be ahead of the antagonism in an ever-changing world in high speeds. Also, employees feel that they are valued by the company and that they are progressing in their careers, something which helps them psychologically and of course professionally. Also, businesses that are using training and strive to empower their employees with new skills and with the latest trends in their industry are the ones most likely to attract the best new employees via their recruitment process.

We can understand from the above that the company culture which has knowledge management attitude embedded in its DNA is the one that will be able to make a difference. In small business this is not always the case as we saw due to lack of resources but in the past years, in many industries, many small businesses understood the importance of adapting a company culture which is enriched by a knowledge management process and striving toward the direction of implementing it.

Small businesses are, in high extent, family owned. This fact per se is very important in terms of the company's culture and creates a very strong connection between the members of the family who are responsible for its implementation and the company's performance as it is derived via the implementation of the company culture in the specific small business. Kellermanns et al. (2010; 2012) stress that many paragons can influence the performance of small businesses, which are family owned. One of them is the relationships between the family members. Kellermanns et al. (2010; 2012) underline that family influence can have both positive and negative consequences on a family-owned company's performance. Such influence can be expressed via the company's culture elements and directions. The CEO of the company is the one responsible for the implementation of the company culture even in small business. In family-owned small business, one characteristic is that the children that come to the CEO's position after the retirement of their parent tend to follow his or her steps. This is usually the case for many reasons. For example, children tend to have their parents as a role model; they admire them and get influenced by them in many ways. Of course, in many cases children tend to go in the opposite direction than their parents in terms of how to manage the company but this is in the minority of the cases. In the author's experience, in family-owned small businesses, the big majority of children tend to follow their parents' steps in terms of how to manage the company in question.

According to Ling et al. (2008), the kind of leadership that small business CEOs express is vital for the company's overall performance and of course for the implementation of the company's culture. As we discussed in the previous chapter, leadership style is a very decisive paragon in terms of the implementation of the company's culture not only in large but also in small businesses. Especially in small business, the less complex context of these firms gives the opportunity to, for example, transformational CEOs to play a more direct role in enhancing the firm's performance via the implementation of the specific company culture which is the result of the mentality of a transformational leader-CEO (Ling et al. 2008).

Ling et al. (2008) in their survey-based research of CEOs in 121 firms and two time-lagged measures of performance, one objective and one perceived, concluded that there is strong linkage between the transformational style of leadership that a small business CEO is exercising and which is depicted in a vivid way via the company's culture and three contingencies which were found to be the following:

- Firm size
- CEO founder status (founder or nonfounder, something which has to do with a CEO who bought the company or a child who inherited it)
- CEO tenure

These characteristics are factors that have vast impact on how the small business CEO will exercise his or her leadership and on how his or her leadership style will be depicted in the company's culture and will affect the company's overall performance.

In support of our sayings in the earlier paragraphs come the results of another research conducted in small business in Norway by Pedersen-Rise and Haddud (2016), which found that family-owned small manufacturing businesses are vastly influenced by the values and beliefs of their founders and owners. Such values and beliefs are the ones that can be found as critical elements and characteristics of the company's culture, the very culture that these founders/owners implement as the CEOs of the company in question. The research was conducted in order to support that implementing lean manufacturing in such small manufacturing companies is something that requires a substantial organizational culture change. Of course, such findings are indicative of the strong influence that the family-owned company's culture has on the company's owner/ CEO. Such influence is critical in the company's culture implementation which needs to change each time we deviate from the owner's philosophy, values, and beliefs.

Another research conducted using an exploratory factor analysis on 779 micro and small companies in Baranquilla in Colombia based on the stakeholder theory[4] by Leon et al. (2017) found that there is very strong influence regarding the company's social responsibility activities that spring from the company's employees, the environment, and the community itself. The research also found that there is weak perception between the companies' owners and managers in terms of undertaking comprehensive programs of social responsibility (Leon et al. 2017). These findings can be interpreted in many ways. The companies' owners are the ones who via their leadership style implement the company culture which might or might not have a social responsibility direction. On the other hand, if the research findings are representative enough, although the specific company cultures are not sensitive enough toward social

---

[4] Stakeholder theory: "Stakeholder theory addresses business ethics, morals and values when managing stakeholders involved with a project or organization. It seeks to optimize relations with stakeholders, thereby improving efficiencies throughout the project or organization" (Blackburn 2019).

responsibility, the companies' employees make the difference as they are sensitive in terms of their social responsibility. This fact per se indicates that company culture in small business has a strong bond with the owners' leadership, vision, and behavior but another crucial paragon that might influence some of the stakeholders (e.g., employees) might be the society in which the company operates.

It is important here to underline that in small societies, in small business, employees usually have a strong bond with the company's owner because they might be relatives or they know each other on personal or family level. This fact is something which creates a different, more complex, bond between them in the business context. Also, even if this is not the case, many times in small business, employees tend to get to know and socialize with each other on a more regular basis. In terms of company culture implementation, although it is derived by the small business owner, employees can sometimes play a critical role as they can influence his or her decisions and sometimes even influence in one or another direction the CEO's leadership style.

Small businesses that operate in small societies (in small cities, villages, etc.) have a strong bond with the societies in which they are operating and this is why when it comes to decision making there are many paragons that the CEOs need to take under consideration that have to do with the company's social responsibility and that have an ethical basis. As the CEOs in such companies are fully responsible for the implementation of the right company culture they need to take under vast consideration such concerns since the local society is very small and they need to maintain a delicate equilibrium between the employees and the society and all these can be achieved via the implementation of the right company culture which needs to have a human-centric direction and focus.

The bottom line is that in small business, company culture is of vast importance and the small business owners need to implement a company culture which needs to be aligned with the societies' ethical considerations. By having a social responsibility mindset, CEOs of small business will be able to achieve such alignment. On the other hand, a very critical point in terms of implementing the company culture that fits best the company in question is the bond that employees might have with the small business' CEO, especially when the company operates in small societies. Ethical consequences might arise on decision level and as such need to be taken under consideration when it comes to the company culture implementation.

The Right Company Culture Implementation in Small Business: How It Can Correlate with Ethical Decision Making—the CEOs' Role

As we already discussed in Chapter 4, company culture is the company's DNA. It can be seen as the way things work inside the company in many terms: from team operations and collaborations, flat organization[5] and open doors that managers might have in order to be able to listen to all ideas, to the ethical standards that the company poses and under which the company in question wants to operate.

Any organization which wants to have an ethical direction in business, a direction that not only has to do with the inside the company operations but also has a social responsibility dimension, needs to implement the right company culture. As we saw in the previous chapter also, such culture can only be derived by the leadership style and the mentality of the company's CEO. This is a fact for both large and small businesses.

In their research, Hiekkataipale and Lämsä (2017; 2019) argue that an insufficient ethical company culture may contribute to indifference in terms of ethical issues that might arise, the experiencing of possible moral conflicts, the lack of self-efficacy, and morally disengaged reasoning.

From the above, we can understand that the implementation of the right company culture in small business is not just a prerequisite in terms of the ethical decision making of the company in question. As the research continues, a "healthy" ethical company culture can be regarded as an asset toward motivation to tackle ethical problems that might arise, not to mention that it can serve as an increased capacity for self-regulation and ultimately for ethical behavior (Hiekkataipale and Lämsä 2017; 2019).

---

[5] Flat organization: "A flat organization refers to an organization structure with few or no levels of management between management and staff level employees. The flat organization supervises employees less while promoting their increased involvement in the decision-making process" (Meehan 2019).

It becomes clear from the results of the above-mentioned research that an ethical and healthy company culture is the cornerstone upon which an ethical decision-making mechanism can be built. As such it can vastly contribute to the ethical decision making of the company's CEO.

Another important factor which vastly influences the implementation of the right company culture in a small business is the company's mission and the employees' commitment to that mission. Each company bears a mission and a vision and both need to be communicated properly and clearly to the company's employees. If this can be achieved, then employees will be able to align their daily activities in a better way with the company's mission and vision. This is crucial and, as Craft and Craft (2018) stress, an intense commitment to the company's mission by the company's employees is a very important element of an ethical company culture.

Since an ethical company can be seen as the base of the ethical decision making and it is derived by the ethical leadership that the company's CEO implements, it should be aligned with the ethical mission and vision of the company. This is why employees' commitment to the company's mission is essential in terms of their alignment with the ethical company culture and the ethical standards upon which the company wants to operate. This kind of behavior will inevitably lead to ethical decision making on a daily basis for both employees and managers when they are facing any kind of decision-making emergency throughout their daily business activities.

As we have already discussed, the leadership style of the CEO is the main factor responsible for the company culture implementation and direction. According to a study conducted by Demitras and Akdogan (2014; 2015), managers can be seen as role models in their organizations. The authors of this research underline that through ethical leadership behavior, managers of all levels can influence perceptions of an ethical culture inside the business climate (Demitras and Akdogan 2014; 2015). In other words, ethical leadership behavior can lead to ethical company culture which is stemmed from ethical behavior in day-to-day operations and actions inside a small business. One of the mainly indirect effects of ethical leadership involves shaping perceptions of an ethical company culture which in result can engender greater affective organizational commitment and less turnover intention from the employees (Demitras and Akdogan 2014; 2015).

> **Ethical leadership → Ethical company culture → Ethical decision making**

Figure 5.1 The road toward ethical decision making

The sequence that leads to ethical decision making in not just small and medium enterprises is given in Figure 5.1.

It is imperative here to underline that an ethical company culture is something that is not easy to be achieved. The debate here is huge: can business be ethical? Everything starts with the CEO's mentality and perspectives. If the CEO wants to take ethical decisions as part of an ethical business philosophy, she needs to operate as a role model for her employees. This leading example of leadership behavior is critical as it will give the right signals to the company's employees and will inspire them toward an ethical direction. As the CEO of the small business is acting in an ethical way and as she will implement an ethical company culture, in order to continue to be consistent with both her mentality, ideas, and vision and the company ethics that she implemented via the company culture, she will be committed in taking ethical decision when the circumstances need them. In addition, unethical behavior which is inconsistent with the company's ethical culture from the part of the employees will not be tolerated as it will create huge negative impact not only on the team but on the company as a whole as the company will start losing her identity.

Ethical decision making on CEO level in small business has to do a lot with the CEO's perspectives in terms of both life and business as part of life. If the CEO's mentality has an ethical direction it will serve accordingly via her leadership the whole organization. According to the author's experience, in many managerial and C-suite positions in many industries in Greece in the last 10 years during the last global financial crisis, as difficult times need difficult decisions, many CEOs were in a dilemma to be ethical or to save their business and survive. In fact, there is no such dilemma but, on the other hand, CEOs are just humans and need to be strong during difficult times and take difficult decisions without compromising their ethical substance. This is something very important because in that way, as they act as role models, they will send the wrong signals to their employees and they will destroy the possible ethical company culture that they have implemented via their ethical leadership during the previous years. In return, an unethical company culture will cultivate a spirit of unethical behavior and will make the company lose its direction and become inconsistent with its vision and mission.

How the Right Business Culture Can Help Small Business to Grow

We saw in both Chapters 3 and 4 that there is huge correlation between company culture, CEO's mentality and leadership style, and ethical decision making. We also discussed about social responsibility and how it can help society increase brand name and, in the long run, increase customer retention and ROI.

The big question, the gist in terms of what bothers business owners, is: How can company culture help small business to grow?

We all know that markets operate based on emotions. For example, if people feel that everything is ok and that the future is bright, they are going to spend money on products of all kinds. On the contrary, if they feel that there is a problem and that their future is going to be difficult or there is any kind of uncertainty, financially or not, they will think twice to spend money on goods and services.

The same goes with the people that work in small business. If they feel right, if they feel respected, if they feel as part of the team, if they have a great work–life balance which leaves them time to spend with their family and friends, then they will be able to walk the extra mile when needed and to deliver exquisite services to their customers. If employees feel great, customers will be feeling great too at the end of the day.

This is something that can be achieved by the implementation of a great company culture, a company culture which will make the people who work in this specific business to feel happy and to be full of positive energy. But then the implementation of such company culture is something, as discussed in the section "The Right Company Culture Implementation in Small Business: How It Can Correlate with Ethical Decision Making—the CEOs' Role," that comes from the head of the small business, the CEO, and it has to do with her leadership style.

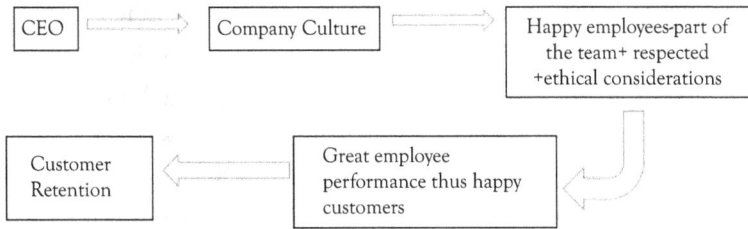

Figure 5.2 From the CEO to increased ROI via company culture

This fact per se is very important as we know that small businesses are the most significant contributor to a nation's job creation, employment (Atanga 2019), and GDP.[6]

In his research, Atanga (2019) underlines that small businesses that focused on their customers' needs and managed to face the challenges that their potential customers were facing were the ones that managed to achieve better sales and customer retention, thus ROI.

From the above, we can understand that what made the difference in that case was that the small businesses that managed to increase their ROI were the ones that had a customer-centric approach. In other words, they were the ones that had the right company culture, the one that valued its customers' needs and was ready anytime to reach them and in that way to create value for them. In such cases, everything again starts from the small business owners. Their approach and leadership style combined with their experience will let them implement the right company culture, the one that will bring value to their customers via the excellent service of the people who are working in that company. The sequence of how this process works is given in Figure 5.2.

In support of our claims in terms of the correlation between the CEO's mentality and leadership style, company culture, and increase in ROI, via increase in sales and customer retention, comes a research that was conducted by Berson et al. (2008). According to this research

---

[6] GDP: "Gross domestic product (GDP) is the total monetary or market value of all the finished goods and services produced within a country's borders in a specific time period. As a broad measure of overall domestic production, it functions as a comprehensive scorecard of a given country's economic health" (Investopedia (3) n.d.).

conducted by gathering data from different sources (26 CEOs, 71 senior vice presidents, 185 other organizational members), CEOs' behavior and even mood vastly relate to organizational outcomes. In addition, CEOs' self-directive values were connected with cultures which were innovation oriented, while security values were associated to bureaucratic cultures and finally, benevolence values were related to cultures which had a supportive character (Berson et al. 2008).

Especially innovative cultures are of utmost importance as they are based on innovation which, as (Manohar and Pandit 2014) indicate, is widely considered as a powerful tool which can be used in stimulating economic growth and in changing the quality of human life. In fact, innovation is the wheel that makes the world go round since the appearance of the first human on the face of the Earth.

We see that CEOs and culture are very strongly connected and that this connection increases growth. On the same wavelength, Parker and Inc Books24×7 (2011; 2012) underlines that CEO's connection to the company culture is extremely valuable for two reasons: first because it gives her the opportunity to define her vision and second because it gives her extremely valuable guidance on how to improve communication throughout the company and, with external stakeholders and customers, on how to set up innovation in a way that it will help the company's growth and of course on how to increase performance. In addition, company culture can help in providing significant shareholder return, in measuring and aligning the organization's efforts and of course in recruiting and retaining the best people in the industry in which the very company operates. Parker and Inc Books24×7 (2011; 2012).

Of course, in small business another important factor that we already examined in this chapter is that the big majority of them are family-owned ones. In family-owned small business there are plenty of elements that create a different bond between the owners and the employees as part of the family-owned company culture which can result in a better outcome. Family loyalty to the company, management style, and mutual trust system, strategic emphasis, criteria for successful business operations, incentives, ongoing process toward continuous improvement, business ethics as part of an ethical company culture, organization, employees' values, employees' satisfaction in terms of operating in the company and under this specific company culture, are important elements that define this specific family owned business approach (Zajec and Roblek 2011).

As we can easily understand, these elements that do not exist in non-family-owned business, at least to that extent, are vital in terms of increasing the possibilities of a high future growth instead of a possible stagnation (Zajec and Roblek 2011). Their existence is interconnected with the implementation of the right company culture which is introduced by the company owner and is followed by both employees and family members that are involved with the business.

Another important aspect in terms of how small businesses can harvest the positive impact of their right company culture and achieve growth is digitalization. Masic et al. (2018) stress that as the world nowadays is becoming more and more digitalized, small business and business as a whole need to adapt in a way that they need to develop a more customer-centric approach in terms of product development (e.g., "customers as innovators"[7] approach), short product cycles, and rapid decision making. In parallel, companies need to develop a more entrepreneurial culture and to build transformational growth engines inside the companies (Masic et al. 2018). In that way, they can tackle their major challenge which is how to implement strategies toward growth and innovation while in parallel they can execute their traditional business model, via the organizational culture and structure which will be aligned with the company's digital transformation (Masic et al. 2018).

We can understand that, as Masic et al. (2018) stress, company culture is the decisive paragon toward transformation in order to achieve growth. Of course, digitalization is of huge importance as well but nothing can be achieved without being implemented via a transformational company culture. Transformation which can be seen as a decisive factor in terms of growth and sustainability, especially for small business, is vastly based upon a transformational company culture.

---

[7] Customers as innovators: "Outsourcing product development to customers" (Thomke and Hippel 2002).

Especially during transformational periods of time not all employees will be happy or able or willing to operate in alignment with the transformational process. As transformation sometimes is a one-way road which if you follow there is no turn back, all employees being aligned with the process is a prerequisite for success. Employees sometimes, on the other hand, might feel overwhelmed by learning new things and by trying hard to adapt to ever-changing situations in their business. Some people also tend to fear about change. This is why in such occasions, the implementation of the right company culture, can be the catalyst toward success and growth.

A great company culture which has both employee-centric and customer-centric focus can motivate employees and make the whole transformation process successful.

Author's Notes

In this chapter we discussed about the role of company culture as described in the previous chapter in the context of small business. We also discussed about how the right positive and ethical company culture need to be implemented in small business and how such culture can correlate with ethical decision making.

We saw the CEO's role in the company culture implementation and analyzed how and why the implementation of the right company culture can help small business grow.

The following topics need to be discussed:

- The role of company culture in the context of small business
- How can we implement the right company culture in a small business
- How the right company culture can impact the ethical decision making in small business
- What the role of the CEO's leadership style and mentality is in the implementation of the right company culture
- How the right company culture implementation can influence positively the company's growth

Questions

1. What is the role of company culture in small business?
2. How can we implement the right company culture in small business?
3. How can company culture impact the decision-making process?
4. What is the role of the CEO in the implementation of the company's culture?
5. Which traits of the CEO's character can play crucial role in company culture implementation?
6. How are company culture and company performance correlated?

PART III

The Gist

CHAPTER 6

Epilogue

Summing Up Our Thoughts: Can Small Business Be Ethical?

Being a small business owner is something thriving and exciting. Owning your company is similar to embarking on an amazing trip which can make you a better person as it will help you understand many things about yourself like your priorities in business and life, your ambitions, your ideas, beliefs and values, and your moral stature.

This very moral stature is the one at stake. Decision making is not something to be taken lightly. It is a paragon that has many implications positive and negative not only for business but for the person that takes the decisions and the society as a whole. What needs to be taken under consideration is that decision making should be based on moral values in order to be supported by the necessary ethical standards and to help not only business to thrive but the society to prosper as well.

Decision makers in small business, need to exercise an ethical leadership which accordingly will be able to implement an ethical company culture. If they are able, as they should, to act as ethical role models, such company culture not only will be possible to be implemented but also will have positive impact on the lives of the people who work in the company and consequently in the society as a whole.

Business owners need to also understand that their company's culture is a paragon which is very influencing in terms of the company's overall performance. It is a factor that will have a huge positive impact on the company's employees who accordingly are going to do the extra mile and excel in their everyday work, something that will also have a huge positive impact on the company's customer satisfaction, thus retention, and of course it will bring an increase in the company's ROI.

In addition, the leadership style that company owners exercise can be crucial as it will be held responsible for the right company culture implementation.

Finally another huge paragon that company owners, especially in small business, need to take under consideration is that they need to follow what the "open systems" theory dictates. As their companies operate as part of a society and as they interact with the society in a two-way interaction, they need to understand that they cannot thrive when society suffocates. Also, they need to understand that nowadays even small businesses operate in a global market and they can address their products on a global scale. This fact per se needs to make them understand that their decisions' implications might have huge global impact on paragons that are so much connected with everybody's lives, like the environment.

Being a leader and a decision maker is not something that can be taken lightly too. It is something huge as the leader's actions and decisions will have vast impact on people's lives inside and outside the company in which the leader operates. Being in a leadership position and not in a managerial one, as leaders and managers are two different options of the same coin, is something that can have major impact on people's lives. It needs to be based on an ethical and a servant leadership base in order to impact positively people's lives via the implementation of a human-centric company culture.

Bottom line? Small businesses can be ethical. In fact, not only they can, but they need to be ethical. Small businesses, as we saw throughout the book, are the backbone of the society and as such their operations and sustainability are crucial not only for them but for the society as well. This is why they need to be ethical. Ethical small businesses mean that they will have a positive moral impact on the societies in which they operate.

Since small businesses are so closely connected to the societies in which they operate, not being ethical will have a devastating result on them and of course on the people who are working for them. For example, when a small manufacturing business operates in a small town, the business itself mainly consists of people who are living in this town. Also there is a huge possibility that the business suppliers will be other small businesses that also operate in the same town. This fact underlines the importance and how crucial every decision is that this small business will take, for example, in terms of ceasing operations and changing its base to a nearby country for lower taxation reasons. Such situation occurred heavily in Greece during the last economic crisis when many small businesses operating in northern Greece ceased operations and relocated to Bulgaria or Skopje because these countries were implementing a lower taxation policy. Although this might seems as something very normal for business and of course it is permitted by the law, in fact it had a huge negative impact on the local societies where the small business in question were operating. They left behind hundreds or even thousands of families with unemployed people, suppliers who suddenly didn't have anywhere to sell their goods so they were forced to go bankrupt, and people who couldn't find specific products and needed to buy them from the surrounding cities/markets at a higher price.

Such situations are completely legal. But are they ethical? Can we baptize as ethical everything that is legal? This is a huge debate and something that business and especially small ones, owners need to take under vast consideration each time they are about to take a decision that will affect the lives of thousands.

Small businesses can be ethical as long as they are based on ethical leadership, a leadership that will be the result of the ethical background of the small business owner. Small business owners need to start the change from within toward their company culture implementation, which can be seen as the cornerstone upon which the company will be able to build its ethical operations. Ethical leadership is the alpha and the omega toward ethical small business.

Since everything starts from the company's CEO, it is imperative that CEOs need to have an ethical mentality which will implement a human-centric approach. The key element of ethical business is the ethical background of the leader/owner/CEO of the company. In addition, the company in question needs to exercise a human-centric approach in terms of how it perceives her customers. Such approach will also be the base for ethical business as sales people won't need to say lies to their customers in order to sell, because all they need to do is to give to their customers what they need and not what the company wants to sell. In that way they will develop with them a transparent relationship and they will be able to add value to them, something which will increase customer retention and will also be able to strengthen the company's brand name in the long run.

Creating value for customers is a key point and as such needs to be treated accordingly by the companies. As customer value proposition is a description of the positive experiences that a target user will realize after purchasing a specific good or receiving a specific service (Hudadoff 2009), it is very important for the company to hear to its customers' needs and ask them, one way or another, what they really need. In that way the company will be able to create or even evolve its profit formula (e.g., customers as innovators).

One of the most important paragons that can determine how customers perceive their value creation is the ethical reasons. For example, they can buy a product which they might not want or use, just in order to contribute in helping their fellow citizens (Best 2014). So, company owners, via their corporate social responsibility, can cultivate an ethical climate between their company and their company's customers as both can be seen as part of the society in which they try to contribute in a positive way. This is the reason why having an ethical profile and adapting a human-centric approach in business is something of so much value and its implementation can be seen as something that gives hope to the society and fulfills employees' and customers' inner moral balance.

So, every small business owner needs to understand beforehand that with power comes responsibility. As they have power over other peoples' lives, they need to use this power in a positive way. In that way their impact to the society as a whole will be huge and this is something that will make a difference and will add meaning to their lives.

References

Al-Tarawneh, K.I. 2020. "Business Ethics in Human Resources Management Practices and its Impact on the Organizational Performance." *Verslas: Teorija Ir Praktika* 21, no. 1, pp. 402–11.

Ammendolia, C., P. Côté, C. Cancelliere, J.D. Cassidy, J. Hartvigsen, E. Boyle, S. Soklaridis, P. Stern, and B. Amick. 2016. "Healthy and Productive Workers: Using Intervention Mapping to Design a Workplace Health Promotion and Wellness Program to Improve Presenteeism." *BMC Public Health* 16, no. 1, p. 1190.

Analoui, F., and A. Karami. 2002. "How Chief Executives' Perception of the Environment Impacts on Company Performance." *Journal of Management Development* 21, no. 4, pp. 290–305.

Antonakis, J., B.J. Avolio, and N. Sivasubramaniam. 2003. "Context and Leadership: An Examination of the Nine-Factor Full-Range Leadership Theory using the Multifactor Leadership Questionnaire." *The Leadership Quarterly* 14, no. 3, pp. 261–95.

Aßländer, M., and T. Goessling. 2017. "Business Ethics, Peace and Environmental Issues." *Journal of Business Ethics* 146, no. 2, pp. 255–56.

Atafar, A., M. Fallahneia, and M.A. Shahrabi. 2013. "A Study on Relationship between Organizational Culture and Productivity." *Management Science Letters* 3, no. 11, pp. 2705–08.

Atanga, J.W. 2019. *Sustainable Business Growth: An Exploration of Ghanaian Small Business Survival.* ProQuest Dissertations Publishing.

Baravska, R. 2016; 2015. "Quality Culture Development in the Industrial Enterprise/Pramonės Įmonių Kokybės Kultūros Plėtojimas." *Science Future of Lithuania* 7, no. 6, pp. 669–8.

Barjzktarović, L., B. Lazarević, and V. Davidović. 2019. "Is Serbian Economy Ready to use Digital Tools in Business Decision-Making Process?" *Industrija (Ekonomski Institut, Beograd)* 47, no. 3, pp. 23–35.

Bartels, L.K., E. Harrick, K. Martell, and D. Strickland. 1998. "The Relationship between Ethical Climate and Ethical Problems within Human Resource Management." *Journal of Business Ethics* 17, no. 7, pp. 799–804.

Berson, Y., S. Oreg, and T. Dvir. 2008. "CEO Values, Organizational Culture and Firm Outcomes." *Journal of Organizational Behavior* 29, no. 5, pp. 615–33.

Best, R. 2014. *Market-Based Management,* 6th ed. Pearson Education Limited. US.

Blackburn, 2019. "Stakeholder Theory." *Projectmanager.com* [blog]. Available at https://projectmanager.com/blog/what-is-stakeholder-theory (accessed on August 25, 2020).

Blackman A., 2018. "What is Ethical Leadership? How to be a Moral Leader." *Business.tutsplus.com* [online]. Available at https://business.tutsplus.com/tutorials/what-is-ethical-leadership--cms-31780 (accessed on August 22, 2020).

Boogaard, K. n.d. "What Kind of Leader Are You? 8 Common Leadership Styles (and Their Pros and Cons)." *Themuse.com* [online]. Available at https://themuse.com/advice/common-leadership-styles-with-pros-and-cons (accessed on August 23, 2020).

Brouthers, K.D., F. Andriessen, and I. Nicolaes. 1998. "Driving Blind: Strategic Decisionmaking in Small Companies." *Long Range Planning* 31, no. 1, pp. 130–38.

Brundin, E., E.F. Samuelsson, L. Melin, Handelshögskolan, Department of Business Administration, Göteborgs universitet, Företagsekonomiska institutionen, Gothenburg University, and School of Business, Economics, and Law. 2014. "Family Ownership Logic: Framing the Core Characteristics of Family Businesses." *Journal of Management & Organization* 20, no. 1, pp. 6–37.

Bulog, I., and I. Grančić. 2017. "The Benefits of Business Ethics - Ethical Behavior of Decision Makers: The Empirical Findings from Croatia." *Mediterranean Journal of Social Sciences* 8, no. 4, pp. 9–14.

Bussmann, K. D., and N. Anja. 2019. "Compliance Through Company Culture and Values: An International Study Based on the Example of Corruption Prevention." *Journal of Business Ethics* 157, no. 3, pp. 797–811.

Çakar, N. D., and A. Ertürk. 2010. "Comparing Innovation Capability of Small and Medium-Sized Enterprises: Examining the Effects of Organizational Culture and Empowerment." *Journal of Small Business Management* 48, no. 3, pp. 325–359.

Caldwell, C., D.X. Truong, P.T. Linh, and A. Tuan. 2010; 2011. "Strategic Human Resource Management as Ethical Stewardship." *Journal of Business Ethics* 98, no. 1, pp. 171–82.

Cancialosi, 2017. "What is Organizational Culture?" *Gothamculture.com* [online]. Available at https://gothamculture.com/what-is-organizational-culture-definition/ (accessed on August 22, 2020).

Cătălina, B. 2008. "Overview on Business Ethics and Human Resources Management Ethics." *Manager* 7, no. 1, pp. 110–13.

Caughron, J.J., A.L. Antes, C.K. Stenmark, C.E. Thiel, X. Wang, and M.D. Mumford. 2011. "Sensemaking Strategies for Ethical Decision Making." *Ethics & Behavior* 21, no. 5, pp. 351–66.

Clements-Croome, D. 2015. "Creative and Productive Workplaces: A Review." *Intelligent Buildings International: Workspaces Promoting Wellbeing* 7, no. 4, pp. 164–83.

Cliffnotes.com, n.d. "Principles of Management." [online]. Available at https://cliffsnotes.com/study-guides/principles-of-management/decision-making-and-problem-solving/the-decisionmaking-process (accessed on July 13, 2020).

Cohen, S.P., S.M. Hayek, S. Datta, Z.H. Bajwa, T.M. Larkin, S. Griffith, G. Hobelmann, P.J. Christo, and R. White. 2010. "Incidence and Root Cause Analysis of Wrong-Site Pain Management Procedures: A Multicenter Study." *Anesthesiology (Philadelphia)* 112, no. 3, pp. 711–18.

Corporatefinanceinstitute.org. n.d. Hofstede's cultural dimensions theory. [online]. Available at https://corporatefinanceinstitute.com/resources/knowledge/other/hofstedes-cultural-dimensions-theory/ (accessed on August 24, 2020).

Corporatefinanceinstitute.org. (2) n.d. "What are the Different Types of Organizations?" [online]. Available at https://corporatefinanceinstitute.com/resources/knowledge/other/types-of-organizations/ (accessed on October 5, 2019).

Craft, J.L., and J.L. Craft. 2018. "Common Thread: The Impact of Mission on Ethical Business Culture. A Case Study." *Journal of Business Ethics* 149, no. 1, pp. 127–45.

Davis, P.S., E. Babakus, P.D. Englis, and T. Pett. 2010. "The Influence of CEO Gender on Market Orientation and Performance in Service Small and Medium-Sized Service Businesses." *Journal of Small Business Management* 48, no. 4, pp. 475–96.

Demirtas, O., and A.A. Akdogan. 2014; 2015. "The Effect of Ethical Leadership Behavior on Ethical Climate, Turnover Intention, and Affective Commitment." *Journal of Business Ethics* 130, no. 1, pp. 59–67.

Detert, J.R., L.K. Treviño, and V.L. Sweitzer. 2008. "Moral Disengagement in Ethical Decision Making: A Study of Antecedents and Outcomes." *Journal of Applied Psychology* 93, no. 2, pp. 374–91.

Dunham, L., J. McVea, and R.E. Freeman. 2008. "Entrepreneurial Wisdom: Incorporating the Ethical and Strategic Dimensions of Entrepreneurial Decision-Making." *International Journal of Entrepreneurship and Small Business* 6, no. 1, pp. 8–19.

Durbin A., 2010. *Leadership. Research, Findings, Practice and Skills*, 6th ed. Cengage Learning. USA.

Ecovadis.com. n.d. "Corporate Social Responsibility." [online]. Available at https://ecovadis.com/academy/corporate-social-responsibility/?campaign=brandads&utm_source=gads&gclid=EAIaIQobChMI2cmjuuS16wIVDKWyCh2Nuw9qEAAYAiAAEgKu_PD_BwE (accessed on August 25, 2020).

Efferin, S., and T. Hopper. 2007. "Management Control, Culture and Ethnicity in a Chinese Indonesian Company." *Accounting, Organizations and Society* 32, no. 3, pp. 223–262.

Fabius, R., R.D. Thayer, D.L. Konicki, C.M. Yarborough, K.W. Peterson, F. Isaac, R.R. Loeppke, B.S. Eisenberg, and M. Dreger. 2013. "The Link between Workforce Health and Safety and the Health of the Bottom Line: Tracking Market Performance of Companies that Nurture a 'Culture of Health'." *Journal of Occupational and Environmental Medicine* 55, no. 9, pp. 993–1000.

Fassin, Y., A. Van Rossem, and M. Buelens. 2011. "Small-Business Owner-Managers' Perceptions of Business Ethics and CSR-Related Concepts." *Journal of Business Ethics* 98, no. 3, pp. 425–53.

Gavin M. 2020. "8 Steps in the Decision Making Process." Online.hbs.edu [online]. Available at https://online.hbs.edu/blog/post/decision-making-process (accessed on July 14, 2020).

Ghattas, J., P. Soffer, and M. Peleg. 2014. "Improving Business Process Decision Making Based on Past Experience." *Decision Support Systems* 59, pp. 93–107.

Gholamzadeh, D., A.T. Khazaneh, and M.S. Nabi. 2014. "The Impact of Leadership Styles on Organizational Culture in Mapsa Company." *Management Science Letters* 4, no. 9, pp. 2161–70.

Goebel, S., S. Goebel, B.E. Weißenberger, and B.E. Weißenberger. 2017. "The Relationship between Informal Controls, Ethical Work Climates, and Organizational Performance." *Journal of Business Ethics* 141, no. 3, pp. 505–28.

Guides.library.Yale.edu. n.d. "Sustainability: Corporate Sustainability." [online]. Available at https://guides.library.yale.edu/c.php?g=296179&p=2582471 (accessed on August 25, 2020).

Hang, X., and C. Wang. 2012. "Strategic Decision-Making in Small and Medium-Sized Enterprises: Evidence from Australia." *International Journal of Business Studies: A Publication of the Faculty of Business Administration, Edith Cowan University* 20, no. 1, pp. 91–110.

Hiekkataipale, M.M., and A.M. Lämsä. 2017; 2019. "(A) Moral Agents in Organisations? the Significance of Ethical Organisation Culture for Middle Managers' Exercise of Moral Agency in Ethical Problems." *Journal of Business Ethics* 155, no. 1, pp. 147–61.

Hofstede, G.H., G.J. Hofstede, and M. Minkov. 2010. *Cultures and Organizations: Software of the Mind.* New York, NY: McGraw-Hill.

Hudadoff P., 2009. "The Customer Value Proposition." *Applied Product Marketing LLC* [pdf]. Available at https://www.engr.colostate.edu/~marchese/stese/reading2.pdf (accessed on November 29, 2015).

Hulpke, J., and C. Lau. 2008. "Business Ethics in China: A Human Resource Management Issue?" *The Chinese Economy* 41, no. 3, pp. 58–67.

Hurst, E., B.W. Pugsley, J. Haltiwanger, and A. Looney. 2011. "What do Small Businesses do [with Comments and Discussion]." *Brookings Papers on Economic Activity* 2011, no. 2, pp. 73–142.

IAEA. 2002. "Ethical Considerations in Protecting the Environment from the Effects of Ionizing Radiation A Report for Discussion [pdf]." Available at https://pub.iaea.org/MTCD/publications/PDF/te_1270_prn.pdf (accessed on July 19, 2020).

Investopedia, (3) n.d. "G.D.P." [online]. Available at https://investopedia.com/terms/g/gdp.asp (accessed on August 26, 2020].

Investopedia, (2) n.d. "Sustainability." [online]. Available at https://investopedia.com/terms/s/sustainability.asp (accessed on August 25, 2020).

Investopedia, n.d. "Enterprise Resource Planning (E.R.P.)." [online]. Available at https://investopedia.com/terms/e/erp.asp (accessed on July 14, 2020).

Jain, A.K., and S. Jain. 2013. "Understanding Organizational Culture and Leadership—Enhance Efficiency and Productivity." *Pranjana: The Journal of Management* 16, no. 2, pp. 43–53.

James, T., G. Anderson and J.R. Katzenbach. 2019. *The Critical Few: Energize Your Company's Culture by Choosing what really Matters.* Oakland: Berrett-Koehler Publishers, Incorporated.

Jocumsen, G. 2004. "How do Small Business Managers make Strategic Marketing Decisions?: A Model of Process." *European Journal of Marketing* 38, nos. 5/6, pp. 659–74.

Jung, Y., and N. Vakharia. 2019. "Open Systems Theory for Arts and Cultural Organizations: Linking Structure and Performance." *The Journal of Arts Management, Law, and Society* 49, no. 4, pp. 257–73.

Karami, A., F. Analoui, and N.K. Kakabadse. 2006. "The CEOs' Characteristics and their Strategy Development in the UK SME Sector: An Empirical Study." *The Journal of Management Development* 25, no. 4, pp. 316–24.

Karaoulanis A., 2015. "The Importance of Management Control Systems." *Journal of Social Sciences Research* 9, no. 1, pp. 1796–99.

Karaoulanis A., 2017. "Financial impediments in risk management mechanisms of Greek Small and Medium Enterprises." *International Journal of Management and Information Technology* 12, no. 1, pp. 3128–52.

Kellermanns, F.W., K.A. Eddleston, R. Sarathy, and F. Murphy. 2010; 2012. "Innovativeness in Family Firms: A Family Influence Perspective." *Small Business Economics* 38, no. 1, pp. 85–101.

Keydifferencies.com. 2017. "Differencies between Formal and Informal Organizations." [online]. Available at https://keydifferences.com/difference-between-formal-and-informal-organization.html (accessed on October 05, 2019).

Klikauer, T. 2017. "Business Ethics as Ideology?" *Critique* 45, nos. 1–2, pp. 81–100.

Klipfolio.com. n.d. "What is a KPI?" [online]. Available at https://klipfolio.com/resources/articles/what-is-a-key-performance-indicator (accessed on July 13, 2020).

Knowledge-management-tools.net. 2018. "Knowledge Management Definition." *Knowledge-management-tools.net* [online]. Available at https://knowledge-management-tools.net/knowledge-management-definition.php (accessed on August 22, 2020).

Kratzer, J., D. Meissner, and V. Roud. 2017. "Open Innovation and Company Culture: Internal Openness Makes the Difference." *Technological Forecasting & Social Change* 119, pp. 128–38.

Kucharska, W., and R. Kowalczyk. 2019. "How to Achieve Sustainability?-Employee's Point of View on Company's Culture and CSR Practice." *Corporate Social-Responsibility and Environmental Management* 26, no. 2, pp. 453–67.

Kuchinke, K.P. 1999. "Leadership and Culture: Work-related Values and Leadership Styles among One Company's U.S. and German Telecommunication Employees." *Human Resource Development Quarterly* 10, no. 2, pp. 135–54.

Lähdesmäki, M., M. Lähdesmäki, M. Siltaoja, M. Siltaoja, L.J. Spence, and L.J. Spence. 2019. "Stakeholder Salience for Small Businesses: A Social Proximity Perspective." *Journal of Business Ethics* 158, no. 2, pp. 373–85.

Lanthier, T. 2016. "Building A Strong, Vibrant Company Culture." *Leadership Excellence Essentials* 33, no. 12, p. 21.

Leković, B., A. Ivanišević, B. Marić, and J.D. Rihter. 2013. "Assessment of the most Significant Impacts of Environment on the Changes in Company Cost Structure." *Economic Research-Ekonomska Istraživanja* 26, no. 1, pp. 225–42.

León, G., H.L.B. Gutiérrez, and J.M.C. Farrero. 2017. "Evaluation of the Perception and Application of Social Responsibility Practices in Micro, Small and Medium Companies in Barranquilla. An Analysis from the Theory of Stakeholders." *Estudios Gerenciales* 33, no. 144, pp. 261–70.

Levine, J. 2018; 2019. *Great Mondays: How to Design a Company Culture Employees Love*, 1st ed. McGraw-Hill Education.

Lincoln S., and A. Holmes. 2011. "Ethical Decision Making: A Process Influenced by Moral Intensity." *Journal of Healthcare, Science and the Humanities* 1, no. 1, pp. 55–59.

Ling, Y., Z. Simsek, M.H. Lubatkin, and J.F. Veiga. 2008. "The Impact of Transformational CEOs on the Performance of Small- to Medium-Sized Firms: Does Organizational Context Matter?" *Journal of Applied Psychology* 93, no. 4, pp. 923–34.

Manohar, S.S., and S.R. Pandit. 2014. "Core Values and Beliefs: A Study of Leading Innovative Organizations." *Journal of Business Ethics* 125, no. 4, pp. 667–80.

Manroop, L., Singh, P., and S. Ezzedeen. 2014. "Human Resource Systems and Ethical Climates: A Resource-Based Perspective." *Human Resource Management* 53, no. 5, pp. 795–816.

Mašić, B., L. Vladušić, and S. Nešić. 2018. "Challenges in Creating Transformative Growth for Companies in Digital Economy." *Economics* 6, no. 2, pp. 37–48.

Meehan, C. 2019. "Flat vs Hierarchical Organizational Structure." [online]. Available at https://smallbusiness.chron.com/flat-vs-hierarchical-organizational-structure-724.html (accessed on December 15, 2020).

Merriam-webster.com n.d. "Social Control." [online]. Available at https://merriam-webster.com/dictionary/social%20control (accessed on August 23, 2020).

Meyer-Galow, E. 2018. *Business Ethics 3.0*, 1st ed. De Gruyter Oldenbourg.

Musbah, A., C.J. Cowton, and D. Tyfa. 2014; 2016. "The Role of Individual Variables, Organizational Variables and Moral Intensity Dimensions in Libyan Management Accountants' Ethical Decision Making." *Journal of Business Ethics* 134, no. 3, pp. 335–58.

Musso, F., and B. Francioni. 2012. "The Influence of Decision-Maker Characteristics on the International Strategic Decision-Making Process: An SME Perspective." *Procedia - Social and Behavioral Sciences* 58, pp. 279–88.

Mustafa, M.A., J. Washbrook, A.C. Lim, Y. Zhou, N.J. Titchener-Hooker, P. Morton, S. Berezenko, and S.S. Farid. 2004. "A Software Tool to Assist Business-Process Decision-Making in the Biopharmaceutical Industry." *Biotechnology Progress* 20, no. 4, pp. 1096–1102.

Octanner.com n.d. "How does Leadership Influence Organizational Culture?" [online]. Available at https://octanner.com/insights/articles/2019/10/23/how_does_leadership_.html (accessed on August 24, 2020).

Ogunyemi, K. 2013. *Responsible Management: Understanding Human Nature, Ethics, and Sustainability*, 1st ed. US: Business Expert Press.

Onu, D., L. Oats, and E. Kirchler. 2018; 2019. "The Dynamics of Internalised and Extrinsic Motivation in the Ethical Decision-Making of Small Business Owners." *Applied Psychology* 68, no. 1, pp. 177–201.

Papke, E. 2013. *True Alignment: Linking Company Culture with Customer Needs for Extraordinary Results*. Nashville: American Management Association.

Parker, M., and Inc Books24×7. 2011; 2012. *Culture Connection: How Developing a Winning Culture Will Give Your Organization a Competitive Advantage*, 1st ed. New York: McGraw-Hill.

Pedersen-Rise, O., and A. Haddud. 2016. "Exploring Lean Culture Challenges in a Small Family-Owned Manufacturing Company: A Case Study from Norway." *International Journal of Lean Enterprise Research* 2, no. 1, pp. 1–25.

Prystupa-Rządca, K. 2017. "The Role of Organizational Culture in Knowledge Management in Small Companies." *Journal of Entrepreneurship, Management and Innovation* 13, no. 3, pp. 151–74.

Purwati, A.S., I. Suparlinah, and N.K. Putri. 2014. "The use of Accounting Information in the Business Decision Making Process on Small and Medium Enterprises in Banyumas Region, Indonesia." *Economy Transdisciplinarity Cognition Journal* 17, no. 2, p. 63.

Reginato, L. and R. Guerreiro. 2013. "Relationships between Environment, Culture, and Management Control Systems." *International Journal of Organizational Analysis* 21, no. 2, pp. 219–40.

Revell, A., D. Stokes, and H. Chen. 2009; 2010. "Small Businesses and the Environment: Turning Over a New Leaf?" *Business Strategy and the Environment* 19, no. 5, pp. 273–88.

Rogers, J. 2017. "Building A Great Company Culture." *Leadership Excellence Essentials* 34, no. 10, pp. 26–27.

Sawabe N. and T. Tobita. 2009. "Roles of Management Control Systems in Organizational Culture." *Melco Journal of Management Accounting Research* 2, no. 1, pp. 53–67.

Skill, ESoft. 2019. *Business Ethics*. Stone River eLearning.

Sonfield, M., R. Lussier, J. Corman, and M. McKinney. 2001. "Gender Comparisons in Strategic Decision-Making: An Empirical Analysis of the Entrepreneurial Strategy Matrix." *Journal of Small Business Management* 39, no. 2, pp. 165–73.

Speer, J. 2019. "What is Quality Culture?" *Greenlight.Guru* [blog]. Available at https://greenlight.guru/blog/quality-culture (accessed on August 25, 2020).

Stakeholdermap.com n.d. "Stakeholder Analysis, Project Management, Templates and Advice." [online]. Available at https://stakeholdermap.com/stakeholder-theory.html (accessed on October 06, 2019).

Surbhi, S. 2018. "Difference Between Morals and Ethics." https://keydifferences.com/difference-between-morals-and-ethics.html (accessed on October 28, 2019).

The-definition.com n.d. "Implementation Control." [online]. Available at https://the-definition.com/term/implementation-control- (accessed on August 23, 2020).

Thomke and Hippel. 2002. "Customers as Innovators:A New Way to Create Value." [online]. Available at https://hbr.org/2002/04/customers-as-innovators-a-new-way-to-create-value (accessed on August 26, 2020).

UKEssays. November 2018. Limiting Factors in a Business Situation. [online]. Available at https://www.ukessays.com/essays/economics/what-sort-of-things-can-become-limiting-factors-in-a-business-situation-economics-essay.php?vref=1 (accessed on December 15, 2020).

Urbandictionary.com n.d. "Micromanagement." [online]. Available at https://urbandictionary.com/define.php?term=micromanagement (accessed on August 24, 2020).

Van Dyck, C., M. Frese, M. Baer, and S. Sonnentag. 2005. "Organizational Error Management Culture and its Impact on Performance: A Two-Study Replication." *Journal of Applied Psychology* 90, no. 6, pp. 1228–40.

Wallstreetmojo.com n.d. "Accounting Controls." [online]. Available at https://wallstreetmojo.com/accounting-controls/ (accessed on August 23, 2020).

Widodo, D.S., and P.E.S. Silitonga. 2017. "Company Performance Analysis: Leadership Style, Corporate Culture and Human Resource Development." *International Review of Management and Marketing* 7, no. 4, pp. 34–41.

Winstanley, D., J. Woodall, and E. Heery. 1996. "Business Ethics and Human Resource Management: Themes and Issues." *Personnel Review* 25, no. 6, pp. 5–12.

Witjes, S., W.J.V. Vermeulen, and J.M. Cramer. 2017. "Exploring Corporate Sustainability Integration into Business Activities. Experiences from 18 Small and Medium Sized Enterprises in the Netherlands." *Journal of Cleaner Production* 153, pp. 528–38.

Wu, T., Y. Wu, H. Tsai, and Y. Li. 2017. "Top Management Teams' Characteristics and Strategic Decision-Making: A Mediation of Risk Perceptions and Mental Models." *Sustainability (Basel, Switzerland)* 9, no. 12, pp. 22–65.

Zajec, M., and M. Roblek. 2011. "Are there Important Differences in Success and in Organizational Culture between Family Companies in Production and Service Sector in Slovenia?" *Organizacija* 44, no. 6, p. 195.

About the Author

Andreas Karaoulanis is a very experienced professional and academic with more than 25 years of experience in many industries, like retail, academia, banking, automotive, insurances, heating and plumbing, apparel and fashion, and start-ups.

He is the author of five books on business topics, three of which have been translated in eight languages.

He is an international lecturer on business topics, an international researcher, and a peer reviewer in many international journals, while he has published a few dozens of scientific research papers which have been read in more than 140 countries all over the world.

He holds a PhD in business management, a master's degree in "decision support and risk analysis", a MBA in industrial management and economics, a master's degree in engineering, and a bachelor's degree in engineering.

Index

OTHER TITLES IN THE ENTREPRENEURSHIP AND SMALL BUSINESS MANAGEMENT COLLECTION

Scott Shane, Case Western University, Editor

- *Blockchain Value* by Olga V. Mack
- *TAP Into Your Potential* by Rick De La Guardia
- *Stop, Change, Grow* by Michael Carter and Karl Shaikh
- *A Cynicâ's Business Wisdom* by Jay J. Silverberg
- *Dynastic Planning* by Walid S. Chiniara
- *From Starting Small to Winning Big* by Shishir Mishra
- *How to Succeed as a Solo Consultant* by Stephen D. Field
- *Small Business Management* by Andreas Karaoulanis
- *Native American Entrepreneurs* by Ron P. Sheffield and Mark J. Munoz
- *The Entrepreneurial Adventure* by David James and Oliver James
- *On All Cylinders, Second Edition* by Ron Robinson
- *Cultivating an Entrepreneurial Mindset* by Tamiko L. Cuellar
- *From Vision to Decision* by Dana K. Dwyer
- *Get on Board* by Olga V. Mack
- *The Rainmaker* by Jacques Magliolo
- *Department of Startup* by Ivan Yong Wei Kit and Sam Lee
- *Family Business Governance* by Keanon J. Alderson

Concise and Applied Business Books

The Collection listed above is one of 30 business subject collections that Business Expert Press has grown to make BEP a premiere publisher of print and digital books. Our concise and applied books are for...

- Professionals and Practitioners
- Faculty who adopt our books for courses
- Librarians who know that BEP's Digital Libraries are a unique way to offer students ebooks to download, not restricted with any digital rights management
- Executive Training Course Leaders
- Business Seminar Organizers

Business Expert Press books are for anyone who needs to dig deeper on business ideas, goals, and solutions to everyday problems. Whether one print book, one ebook, or buying a digital library of 110 ebooks, we remain the affordable and smart way to be business smart. For more information, please visit www.businessexpertpress.com, or contact sales@businessexpertpress.com.

www.ingramcontent.com/pod-product-compliance
Lightning Source LLC
Chambersburg PA
CBHW061830220326
41599CB00027B/5241